THE GUIDE CIGARETTE COLLECTING

1993 VALUES
NINETEENTH REVISED EDITION

Compiled and published by:

ALBERT'S THE CIGARETTE CARD SPECIALISTS

Head Office & Showrooms
113 LONDON ROAD, TWICKENHAM TW1 1EE
Telephone 081-891 3067

OPEN	TUESDAY to FRIDAY	10 a.m. — 6 p.m.
	SATURDAY	10 a.m. — 4 p.m.

ISBN 0 946644 09 8

Published by : Albert's The Cigarette Card Specialists
Printed by: Rayment Printers Limited, 5 Horsham Road, Dorking, Surrey.
Telephone (0306) 886198   Fax: (0306) 742148

CONTENTS

	Page
Foreward	4
How to Use the Catalogue	4/5
Introduction	6/7
A Brief History of Cigarette Cards	7, 173/174
Albert's Postal Auctions	8
Gift Vouchers	9
Cigarette Card Albums	10/11
Frames	12
Cigarette Card Mixtures	13
Albert's Shop (The Golden Oldies)	14
Abbreviations	15
Makers, Set Names Dates Prices and Card Illustrations	16/172
Collecting for Pleasure and Investment	174/176
Cigarette Cards of Other Countries	176/178
Misprints and Variations	178/181
Cigarette Card Novelties	181/182
Trade Cards	182/184
Cigarette Card Storage	184/186
Index of Tobacco Brand Names	187/192
Notes	192

FOREWORD

It is with great pleasure that we present the 19th Revised Edition of our Cigarette Card Guide and Catalogue.

Although the past year has been a very difficult one for most businesses, Cigarette Cards have come through remarkably well.

Collectors, like everyone else, have had to restrict their spending, so naturally there has not been the staggering price increases we have seen in recent years. However, the enthusiasm has been as keen as ever and we are pleased to report another very successful year.

Our Twickenham Shop "THE GOLDEN OLDIES" has become *a Popular Venue* for both Collector's and Customer's *seeking UNIQUE GIFTS* with thousands of *unusual items* on view in glass display cabinets — mostly ranging from 50 to 100 years old including hundreds of sets of Cigarette Cards, Vanity Fair Prints, Automotons, Music Boxes, Hand-made Models, Military Figures, Old Comics, Film Magazines, Annuals, Jig-Saws, Film Mobilia, etc., etc.

Collectors old and new will find a visit to our Twickenham Shop (The Golden Oldies) of interest and are welcome to browse through our range of display albums before choosing sets.

Collectors unable to call personally will find our Mail Order Department second to none. VISA and ACCESS card holders can telephone 081-891 3067 during opening hours with orders which will be dispatched the same day.

HOW TO USE THE CATALOGUE

Our catalogue gives an accurate guide to the value of cards, as our unique grading system enables a collections value to be assessed correctly, according to condition.

We have a very extensive range of sets, however, as stocks change daily it is always advisable to list alternatives when ordering.

Column 1 — Ref No: This saves collectors the tiresome business of listing by name the sets required.

Example:—

Maker	Ref. No.:	Price
Players	187	
Wills	9	

ETC:—

Where there is no Reference Number beside the set, this means it is unlikely to be in stock.

Column 2 — Number in Set & Size This tells you how many cards are in the set and the size of the cards.

If there is no letter preceding the number the cards are Standard Size and fit into the A Size Pockets.

Other letters used are M.L.X.P.S. these sizes correspond to the various size pockets, used with the De-Luxe Albums. (For further details — see pages 10 and 11.) Z Size means the cards are too large for albums.

Column 3 — Name of Set Most sets have the name of the set on the back of the card, where this does not apply the set has been given an adopted title. (These titles are accepted throughout the hobby.)

(F) after title means the set is photographic.

(ST) means stereoscopic.

Column 4. — Date.   This is the approximate year the set was issued.

Columns 5 & 6 — Grades   **GRADE 2**   Good collectable condition, cards acceptable to all our customers who do not specialise in grade 1 sets.

        GRADE 1   Excellent — Mint condition sets (naturally stocks are low on this grade).

When ordering please indicate your preference to Grade, and whether you will accept either.

TERMS OF BUSINESS
(All previous prices cancelled)

Cash with Order.   Cheques, Money Orders or Postal Orders should be made payable to: ALBERT's and crossed. Cash should always be Registered.

Orders are accepeted over the telephone and dispatched within 24 hours to customers using Access and Visa Cards.

Postage and Package.   Postage is charged at current Inland or Overseas Postal Rates. As these are constantly changing we ask customers to estimate the cost, and any small debit or credit will be carried forward to your next order.

OUR GUARANTEE   All orders are privately insured and the nominal charge for this service is added to the Postal Charges. Substantial orders will be registered.

VAT   If applicable, is included in all our prices.

BACK NUMBERS
(Useful for assessing how values have increased)

Most editions are now out of stock. However, we do have a limited amount of 1982, 1983 and 1984 at £3 each, 1985, 1986, 1987, 1988, 1989, 1990, 1991 and 1992 at £4 each, or all eleven years for £32.00.

ALBUM SALES
See Pages 10 and 11.

Request for Information or Quotations should always be accompanied by a Stamped Addressed Envelope.

PURCHASING
We are always prepared to purchase collector's unwanted sets. Please write giving details before sending your cards — Thank you.

MAIL ORDER DEPT: ALBERT'S THE CIGARETTE CARD SPECIALISTS
113 LONDON ROAD, TWICKENHAM TW1 1EE
Tel: 081-891 3067 ANSWER PHONE SERVICE OUTSIDE OFFICE HOURS
ENABLING CUSTOMERS TO PLACE ORDERS ANY TIME DAY OR NIGHT.

CALLERS WELCOME
TUESDAY to FRIDAY   10 a.m.—6 p.m.
SATURDAY   10 a.m.—4 p.m.

INTRODUCTION

If you were able to travel back through time, even only as far back as the years immediately following the Second World War, you would come across a way of life that has vanished from the present scene. Examine − if your nerves and stomach are strong enough! − the contents of a young lad's pockets. Conkers, a few boiled sweets, (only a few because of sweet rationing), a marble or two maybe even a lead soldier . . . and cigarette cards.

These colourful and varied pieces of card with their highly individualistic pictures, portraits and scenes, were an integral part of a boy's life. Many a nose had been bloodied or a milk tooth prematurely ejected for the recovery or possession of the elusive card which would complete the set.

It was an everyday sight in any school playground. Two boys kneeling side by side, flicking cards against the wall. Any card which was covered by another was won. As simple as that. A hard 'sudden death' game, surely as cut throat as any Poker school. You only had to look at those intense young faces to realize that.

And there were the onlookers. Those who enjoyed to watch as critical spectators, vicariously sharing in the joys of the winner or the disappointment of the loser.It was mirrored in their faces, and it was a part of their young lives that they would never forget. Alas, today's child is all the poorer for being deprived of the ups-and-downs, the put-and-take fortunes and misfortunes of cigarette cards.

Unfortunately, at that time there were no new sets being produced as the war had caused a paper shortage. Most serious adult collectors were either overseas or completely involved in some way or another with the war and its aftermath.

World War II was responsible for the destruction of vast amounts of cigarette cards, and sadly many collectors returned home to find their collections destroyed by the bombing.

Huge quantities of cards were gathered for waste paper and even dealers disposed of all, or, large amounts of their stocks to be pulped.

These factors, plus the countless millions of cards which were flicked up against the walls in school playgrounds throughout the country during the thirties and forties inevitably contributed a great deal to the shortage of sets available today.

Prior to the war cigarette cards flourished in popularity. There were those who played and those who collected, but the collecting was a somewhat more complex business. Dad or an older brother were a useful source of supply − if they smoked. Or else it could mean keeping on good terms with an older sister's boyfriend(s). Should that be of no avail the young pre-war collector would be found loitering outside tobacconist shops, ready to pounce on the unwary customer with a plea of, "please, mister, got any fag cards?"

A major part of the appeal that cigarette cards held for adult collectors at this time could probably be put down to the widening of horizons that they brought to the ordinary man (sorry, person!) in the street. They became a way of life, much the same as the football pools and the telly have. And it could well be due to such things as television that cigarette card production has never been resumed.

In those byegone days cigarette card collecting was generally regarded by most people as little more than a passing phase. How often we now hear those sceptics crying out in forlorn hindsight, "if we had only known, we would never have thrown them away!"

Today, men — and increasingly women, too — from all walks of life, are avid collectors. And the number of collectors is very much on the increase as the hobby continues to gain status. The fact that cigarette card collecting has survived for over a century despite the fact that very few sets have been issued since 1939 surely indicates that the sceptics have been proved wrong.

In recent years we have had various substitutes in bubble gum and other similar products but they lacked the appeal, the subtle 'something' that made cigarette cards that bit more special.

As far as the return of cigarette cards goes, well, the circumstances are not particularly favourable. The recent swing to anti-smoking doesn't exactly herald their return and the link with lung cancer and cigarettes obviously imposes its own restrictions on the re-emergence of cigarette cards.

But it seems to be generally accepted that cigars are less harmful than cigarettes, and the manufacturers give indication of moving in this direction in most of their advertising promotions. And cards are no exception. In 1975 John Player issued a set called 'The Golden Age of Motoring' with Doncella Cigars, and since then they have issued a number of series. In 1979 they extended their promotion to Grandee Cigars. More recently their Tom Thumb Cigars are also carrying on the good work, and Wills have also hopped onto the bandwagon in the shape of their Embassy Cigars. This means that there are now two major tobacco manufacturers issuing cards in four different brands. These sets are, in the main, very well illustrated with good text on the back and are considered by most collectors to be very collectable.

However, because of their imposed limits, cigarette cards have become all that more precious. There is an almost esoteric appeal – a mystique that many of us still remember from our schooldays. Some collectors take their hobby to such painstaking degrees as noting, for example, variations in the printing on the back in much the same way that the stamp collector would check for the differences in watermarks. This in itself is highly commendable, but for the dyed-in-the-wool cigarette card collector – or cartophilist, to use the correct term – the hunting and searching and finally tracking down of that long sought after set is pleasure enough. Never mind all the technicalities. The set's the thing! The collector-enthusiast isn't going to take the rainbow to pieces to see how it is made. He is more than happy to appreciate the rainbow in its entirety.

(II)

A BRIEF HISTORY OF CIGARETTE CARDS

When was the first cigarette card issued? Who thought up the idea, and who, in fact, issued them? These are all mysteries that still remain unasnwered. We can, however, be more specific by stating that they were first issued in America and that their origins date back over one hundred years. Truly the history of cartophily – cigarette card collecting – is an intriguing one.

It is a known fact that as far back as the 1860s many tradesmen advertised every commodity imaginable on picture cards which they gave away to their customers. It is therefore not unreasonable to suppose that these were also issued with cigarettes, although this cannot be confirmed to date. Still others believe that Robert Peacock Gloag may have used cigarette cards as early as the Crimea War Period (1854).

Over the years many articles have appeared in the newspapers stating that the first cigarette card on official record was produced for the Marquis of Lorne cigarettes in America in 1878, featuring a portrait, presumably of the Marquis of Lorne himself.

Another popular story is that in around 1878, one Edward Bok, a famous American journalist, was out walking one day when he picked·up a cigarette card that had been dropped in the street, showing a picture of an actress of that particular time. The reverse side of the card was blank, and Mr. Bok, being a man of words, hit upon the idea of putting text on the back. Although this story cannot be verified, Mr. Bok has been credited with this stage in the development of cigarette cards.

Continued on page 173

7

ALBERT'S Postal Auctions

Lots on view at our shops — one week prior to Auction.

200-300 Lots per Auction including many rare items.

Cigarette & Trade cards, Ephemera, Movie Magazines, Annuals, Stills, Lead Figure Comics, etc.

SPECIAL OFFER

New subscribers to our Auctions will receive 50 free cigarette cards (our choice).

The cost of producing Auction Catalogues for one year, printing, addressing, postage etc., is approximately £8, per subscriber.

When you pay £4.00 (UK postage included), you will receive our Auction Catalogues for one year — providing you are placing Successful Bids.

We cannot however, continue to subsidise collectors who wish to obtain our Auction Catalogues for reference only. Therefore subscribers who have not placed successful bids within six months will automatically be taken off our auction list.

Alternatively, subscribers who do not intend bidding may send £8, for one year's subscription.

(AVERAGE 10-11 AUCTIONS A YEAR)

ALBERT'S GIFT VOUCHERS
ALWAYS APPROPRIATE FOR ANY OCCASION
Attractive gold foil greeting card with envelope inscribed "For You"

Gift Voucher

A Gift For _____

Worth _____ Pounds £ [   ]

From _____

Authorised By _____ Expires _____

ALBERT'S CIGARETTE CARD SPECIALISTS
113 London Road
TWICKENHAM. TW1 1EE
Telephone: 081 891 3067

On numerous occasions over the years, we have encountered the problem of collectors wives, friends and relations trying to purchase a gift, but not knowing where to begin.

The Introduction of the ALBERT'S GIFT VOUCHER solves this problem once and for all. VOUCHERS MAY BE FOR ANY SUM YOU REQUIRE EXCEEDING £10.

No charge is made for the actual GREETING CARD and ENVELOPE — just for the amount you require the gift to be.

The GIFT VOUCHER can be used for any item listed in the Albert Guide, for payment or part payment in ALBERT'S Auctions, or at OUR SHOP "The Golden Oldies" with a unique stock of 40,000 sets of Cigarette Cards, Albums, Frames and Accessories plus old Film Magazines, Stills, Comics, Jig Saws, Prints, Music Boxes, Gramophones, Military Figures, Wild Life Sculptures, Model Cars, Trains, Ships, Brasses, etc., etc.

HOW TO OBTAIN AN ALBERT'S GIFT VOUCHER
Simply supply us with the name of the person you want the Gift Voucher made out too, how much it is for and your name.

TELEPHONE: 081-891 3067 with your VISA/ACCESS Number and your GIFT VOUCHER will be sent by post the same day.

BY POST;   Send a cheque, money order, postal order, etc., made payable to Albert's. Alternatively give your ACCESS/VISA number and expiry date or send registered cash.

PERSONALLY: CALL INTO OUR SHOP.
Hours of Business: Tues-Fri 10am-6pm
Saturday 10am-4pm

9

ALBERT'S ALBUMS

Our album leaves have been tested on our behalf by laboratories recommended by I.C.I., thus assuring there will be no harmful effects to your collection.

All Leaves	13p each
Album Cover and Album Slip Cover (weight 800 grams)	£ 6.25
Black Backing Sheets (weight 300 grams) (pack of 40)	£ 1.90

SPECIAL OFFER A

Cover and Slip Cover	£ 6.25
40 Leaves	£ 5.20
40 Black Backing Sheets	£ 1.90
	£13.35
SAVE	£ 2.35
PAY	£11.00 plus postage (1½ kilo)

Covers and Slip Covers in Green, Blue, Maroon, Tan and Dark Brown.

SPECIAL OFFER B

500 Black Backing Sheets	£23.75
SAVE	£ 3.00
PAY	£20.00 plus postage (4 kilo)

SPECIAL OFFER C

100 Leaves for £12.00 (Save £1.00) plus postage (1½ kilo)

Plus Postage — As this is constantly changing we have shown the weights of the item(s).

Alternatively you may estimate the postage and we will debit or credit you.

ALBERT'S ALBUMS

YOUR COLLECTION DESERVES THE BEST

COVERS & SLIP COVERS in Five Colours, Green, Blue, Maroon, Tan & Dark Brown.

Black Backing Sheets: These Backing Sheets are the same size as our album leaves punched to interleave in your album. They will make your cards stand out more thus enhancing your collection.

Leaves to hold the following card sizes are available:-

Size		Maximum Size Card each Pocket will Hold		
A	has	10 Pockets	80 x 41 mm	(Standard Size Vertical Cards)
M	has	8 Pockets	80 x 52 mm	(Medium Size Cards)
L	has	6 Pockets	80 x 71 mm	(Large Size Cards)
D	has	6 Pockets	105 x 55 mm	(Doncella Cigar Size Cards)
X	has	4 Pockets	80 x 107 mm	(Extra Long Size Cards)
P	has	2 Pockets	168 x 105 mm	(Post Card Size Cards)
S	has	1 Pocket	168 x 220 mm	(Cabinet Size Cards)

See opposite page for Prices.

11

ALBERT'S FRAMED CIGARETTE CARDS
THE IDEAL DISPLAY OR PRESENT

The choice is yours, we will frame your cards without damage or you can purchase a "Do It Yourself Kit".

Wide range of subjects over 40,000 sets in stock.

Do It Yourself Kits comprising of wooden frame, cut out mounting board, spring clips, rings & screws currently in eight formats, others to follow.

Size One	to hold 50 Standard size cards Vertical (5 cards across, 10 down)
Size Three	to hold 50 Black Cat (10 cards across, 5 down)
Size Four	to hold 25 Standard size card Vertical
Size Five	to hold 25 Large size cards
Size Six	to hold 48 Gailaher cards Vertical
Size Seven	to hold 50 Standard size cards Vertical (10 cards across, 5 down)
Size Eight	to hold 10 Standard size cards Vertical (2 cards across, 5 down)

All vertical frames horizontal if turned sideways.

KITS

Size	4	£15.99 each	
Size	1-3, 5, 6, or 7	£23.99	
Size	8	£ 8.99 each	plus postage

Mounting Boards can be sent through the post, but a minimum order of 10 boards.

Size	4	£2.99 each	
Size	1-3, 5, 6 or 7	£3.99 each	
Size	8	£1.50 each	plus postage

Glass for frames 50p — £3.00 per sheet — Callers only.

Complete Framing Service — Callers only.

POSTAGE — As this is constantly changing — simply add £3.50 to your order and we will debit or credit you accordingly.

For
Collectors who
prefer the fun of making
up their own sets

220
CIGARETTE CARDS

£21.00

+ £1.50 postage & insurance

This Mixture will contain cards from
many different sets, and although condition will vary from poor to mint, we do
guarantee value for money, and the
majority of cards are in Good Collectable
Condition.

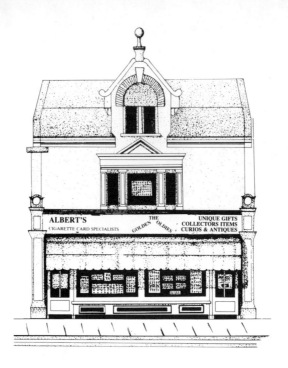

COLLECTORS ARE INVITED TO VISIT ALBERT'S UNIQUE SHOP
THE GOLDEN OLDIES
ALSO
MAIL ORDER DEPARTMENT AND HEAD OFFICE

Tel: 081-891 3067 with your ACCESS or VISA Card Number and your Order will be dispatched the same day.

Stocks comprise of approximately 40,000 sets, the Finest Cigarette Card Albums & Accessories on the market, Frames for Cards, Guides etc.

Plus thousands of Film Magazines and Comics ranging from Pre World War 1 to 1960's, original Vanity Fair prints dating back to 1869, 19th Century Jig-Saws, Film Stills, Laurel & Hardy Memorabilia (Sons of the Desert Welcomed), Automatons, collectors hand painted lead and pewter figures, Myth and Magic Stockists.

We now have full time artists who specialise in top quality hand painted Military Figures and Sculptures.

Why not pay us a visit and view our unique range of Collector's Items, Gifts, Curios and Antiques.

THE IDEAL GIFT — AN ALBERT'S GIFT VOUCHER — See Page 9

To get to The Golden Oldies — come out of Twickenham Station, turn right and our premises are facing you.

Bus routes that go to Twickenham Station: 267. 110. 281.

Bus routes which are within 5 minutes walking distance of Twickenham Station: 33. 90b. 202. 270. 290.

ALBERT'S THE CIGARETTE CARD SPECIALISTS
113 London Road, Twickenham TW1 1EE. Tel: 081-891 3067

Hours of Opening: Tuesday—Friday 10am—6pm   Saturday 10am—4pm

ABBREVIATIONS used throughout this publication

Excluding code letters used after some early sets of Actresses, Beauties, etc., which indicate where identical sets were issued by several firms.

A.A.	As Above – this means the set is as the above set e.g. Wills "First Aid" set 220 & 281 are the same except for the Album Clause on the back of set 220.
AUST.	Australia.
A/C.	Album Clause.
ANON.	Anonymous – no makers or brand names on the cards.
B & W.	Black & White.
CAPS.	Captions.
C.Is.	Channel Isles.
CIGS.	Cigarettes.
COL.	Coloured.
CON'T.D.	Continued.
DIFF.	Different.
F/L	Frame Lines.
F.	Photographic
F-ST.	Photographic Stereoscopic.
HORZ.	Horizontal
I.A.	Including Above – meaning that the cards in the above set are included.
I.T.C.	Imperial Tobacco Company.
L. & B.	Lambert & Butler.
LTD.	Limited.
Nd.	Numbered.
N.Z.	New Zealand.
OVS.	Overseas.
PAT.	Patent.
P/B.	Plain Back.
P/C.	Playing Card.
PORTS.	Portraits.
PROV.	Provisional.
S.A.	South Africa.
SECT.	Sectional.
S.T.A.	Similar to Above – possibly one or two cards different.
TOB.	Tobacco.
Un.Nd.	Un-Numbered.
VERT.	Vertical.

This Catalogue is devoted entirely to cards issued by the Tobacco Firms. When ordering please write — makers name, reference number and preference to Grade.

To Avoid Possible Disappointment Please List Alternatives

Details of Grading on Page 5.

Ref. No.	No. in Set	Name of Set	Date	COMPLETE SETS Grade 1	Grade 2
		ABDULLA & CO. LTD.			
	50	Beauties of Today	1938	260.00	160.00
1626	25	British Butterflies	1935	28.00	18.00
	?4	Bridge Rule Cards	1925	100.00	50.00
	52	Cinema Stars Set 1(F)	1932	260.00	160.00
	30	Cinema Stars Set 2	1932	200.00	120.00
	30	Cinema Stars Set 3	1933	160.00	100.00
5255	32	Cinema Stars Set 4	1933	85.00	55.00
3424	32	Cinema Stars Set 5	1934	85.00	55.00
	30	Cinema Stars Set 6	1934	135.00	90.00
615	25	Feathered Friends	1935	28.00	14.00
	50	Film Favourites	1934	260.00	160.00
	50	Film Stars	1934	430.00	280.00
	P24	Film Stars (Series of Cards, Postcard Back)	1934	260.00	160.00
	P24	Film Stars (Series of Cards. Non Postcard Back) A.A.	1934	260.00	160.00
	P24	Film Stars (Series of 24 Cards. Postcard Back)	1934	260.00	160.00
	P24	Film Stars (Series of 24 Cards Non Postcard Back) A.A.	1934	260.00	160.00
	P24	Film Stars, 2nd (25-48 Postcard Back)	1934	260.00	160.00
	18	Message Cards (Alphabet Letters)	1936	165.00	110.00
	K18	Message Cards (Alphabet Letters)	1936	240.00	160.00
616	25	Old Favourites (Flowers)	1936	32.00	16.00
	L1	Princess Mary Gift Card	1914	28.00	14.00
522	40	Screen Stars (Abdulla Back)	1939	60.00	40.00
	40	Screen Stars (back, by the Successors) A.A.	1939	90.00	60.00
	50	Stage and Cinema Beauties	1935	200.00	130.00
	30	Stars of The Stage and Screen	1934	160.00	100.00

Ref. No.	No. in Set	Name of Set	Date	COMPLETE SETS Grade 1	Grade 2
		ADCOCK & SON			
	12	Ancient Norwich	1928	75.00	50.00
1394	11/12	Ancient Norwich (No.6 scarce) A.A.	1928	45.00	30.00
		ADKIN & SON			
	25	Actresses (Numbered 126-150)	1898	—	—
3887	12	A Living Picture (Adkin & Sons)	1901	130.00	65.00
	12	A Living Picture (back, these cards are) A.A.	1901	130.00	65.00
	X12	A Living Picture (premium issue)	1901	1200.00	600.00
2284	12	A Royal Favourite	1900	300.00	150.00
	15	Beauties (PAC)	1899	—	—
3263	50	Butterflies & Moths	1924	115.00	65.00
5411	12	Character Sketches (black back)	1901	130.00	65.00
289	12	Character Sketches (green back) A.A.	1901	130.00	65.00
	X12	Character Sketches (premium issue)	1901	1200.00	600.00
	?4	Games — By Tom Brown	—	—	—
1539	25	Notabilities	1915	180.00	90.00
	12	Pretty Girl Series (Actresses)	1898	950.00	475.00
	12	Pretty Girl Series (RASH)	1899	550.00	275.00
3239	50	Soldiers of The Queen	1899	340.00	170.00
683	59	Soldiers of The Queen (Series of 60 on back)	1900	400.00	200.00
	31	Soldiers of The Queen & Portraits	1901	260.00	130.00
	30	Sporting Cups & Trophies	1914	850.00	425.00
3370	25	War Trophies	1917	200.00	100.00
499	50	Wild Animals of the World	1923	90.00	60.00
		PHILIP ALLMAN & CO. LTD.			
476	50	Coronation Series	1953	33.00	22.00
3169	12	Pin-Up Girls 1st Series (Nd)	1953	42.00	28.00
757	12	Pin-Up Girls 1st Series (Un Nd for men only) A.A.	1953	42.00	28.00
927	12	Pin-Up Girls 1st Series (Un Nd Ask for Allman always) A.A.	1953	45.00	30.00
2571	L12	Pin-Up Girls 1st Series A.A.	1953	57.00	38.00
3281	12	Pin-Up Girls 2nd Series	1953	45.00	30.00
2572	L12	Pin-Up Girls 2nd Series A.A.	1953	57.00	38.00

Ref. No.	No. in Set	Name of Set	Date	COMPLETE SETS Grade 1	Grade 2
		E. & W. ANSTIE LTD.			
4014	25	Aesop's Fables	1934	65.00	42.00
4088	16	British Empire Series	1904	300.00	150.00
2132	10	Clifton Suspension Bridge (Sectional)	1938	21.00	14.00
	B?40	Flags (Silk)	1916	84.00	42.00
	X?9	Flags (Silk)	1916	130.00	65.00
	40	Nature Notes	1939	280.00	150.00
2861	50	People of Africa	1926	300.00	150.00
2793	50	People of Asia	1926	300.00	150.00
3109	50	People of Europe	1925	260.00	130.00
2134	40	Places of Interest	1939	30.00	20.00
	8	Puzzle Series	1902	1200.00	600.00
2941	50	Racing Series	1922	320.00	160.00
	?82	Regimental Badges (Silk)	1916	230.00	115.00
5646	M5	Royal Mail Series	1899	1600.00	800.00
	X5	Royal Standard & Portraits (Silk)	1916	340.00	170.00
2593	50	Scout Series	1923	190.00	95.00
2171	10	Stonehenge (Sectional)	1936	21.00	14.00
2172	10	The Victory (Sectional)	1936	18.00	12.00
3110	50	The World's Wonders	1924	90.00	60.00
2173	20	Wells Cathedral (Sectional)	1935	36.00	24.00
3300	40	Wessex	1938	48.00	32.00
2174	20	Wiltshire Downs (Sectional)	1935	36.00	24.00
2175	10	Windsor Castle (Sectional)	1937	18.00	12.00
		HENRY ARCHER & CO.			
	26	Actresses (FROGA) (back Golden Returns)	1901	2400.00	1200.00
	26	Actresses (FROGA) (back M.F.H.) A.A.	1901	2400.00	1200.00
5565	50	Beauties (CHOAB) (brown front Bound to Win)	1901	2200.00	1100.00
	50	Beauties (CHOAB) (coloured Golden Returns) A.A.	1901	5600.00	2800.00
	50	Beauties (CHOAB) (coloured M.F.H.) A.A.	1901	5600.00	2800.00
1541	20	Prince of Wales	1900	900.00	450.00

A SELECTION OF CRICKET SETS

CARRERAS
SET 3767

SET 354

CARRERAS
SET 3013

DRAPKIN
SET 362

GALLAHER
SET 1799

SET 179

SET 348

SET 2262

SET 1919

Ref. No.	No. in Set	Name of Set	Date	COMPLETE SETS Grade 1	Grade 2
		ARDATH TOBACCO CO. LTD.			
	50	Animals at The Zoo (Export descriptive text back)	1924	150.00	100.00
	50	Animals at the Zoo (Export Double Ace back) A.A.	1924	790.00	525.00
	50	Beautiful English Women (Export)	1930	170.00	110.00
	25	Big Game Hunting (Export black back)	1930	300.00	200.00
	25	Big Game Hunting (Export blue back) A.A.	1930	115.00	75.00
	L30	Boucher Series (Export)	1915	150.00	75.00
1084	50	Britain's Defenders	1936	55.00	35.00
3267	50	British Born Film Stars (Export)	1934	85.00	55.00
	M50	British Born Film Stars (Export) A.A.	1934	135.00	90.00
	50	Butterflies (Ladies) (Export)	1932	—	—
	P1	Calendar (Silk)	1937	—	—
	X1	Calendar 1942	1941	4.00	2.00
	X1	Calendar 1942-3	1942	4.00	2.00
	X1	Calendar 1943	1942	5.00	2.50
	X1	Calendar 1943-4	1943	3.00	1.50
	X1	Calendar 1944	1943	3.00	1.50
3890	36	Camera Studies (F)	1939	55.00	35.00
701	L45	Camera Studies (F)	1939	60.00	40.00
1973	X25	Champion Dogs	1934	40.00	25.00
	X100	Contract Bridge Contest Hands (folders)	1930	—	—
491	50	Cricket, Tennis & Golf Celebrities	1935	84.00	42.00
	150	Do You Know	1938	—	—
	X25	Dog Studies (Ardath at base-export)	1938	225.00	150.00
2176	X25	Dog Studies (State Express) A.A.	1938	85.00	55.00
	25	Dutch Scenes (Export)	1928	—	—
	25	Eastern Proverbs (Export)	1932	45.00	30.00
2416	48	Empire Flying Boat (Sectional)	1938	110.00	70.00
427	50	Empire Personalities	1937	50.00	30.00
13	50	Famous Film Stars	1934	56.00	36.00
14	50	Famous Footballers	1934	80.00	40.00
1508	25	Famous Scots	1935	27.00	18.00
1879	X25	Fighting & Civil Aircraft	1936	48.00	32.00
541	50	Figures of Speech	1936	80.00	40.00
453	50	Film, Stage & Radio Stars	1935	80.00	40.00
1974	X25	Film, Stage & Radio Stars (Different)	1935	36.00	24.00
	M50	Flags 4th Series (Silk. Dutch text)	1914	—	—
	M50	Flags 5th Series (Silk. Dutch text)	1915	—	—
	25	Flags 6th Series (Silk. Dutch text)	1915	—	—

A SELECTION FROM ARDATH

SET No: 1974

SET No: 427

SET No: 491

SET No: 1085

SET No: 14

SET No: 541

SET No: 13

SET No: 1973

Ref. No.	No. in Set	Name of Set	Date	COMPLETE SETS Grade 1	Grade 2
		ARDATH TOBACCO CO. LTD. (Cont'd)			
	L40	Franz Hals Series (Dutch Back)	1916	920.00	460.00
844	X50	From Screen & Stage	1936	45.00	30.00
	L30	Gainsborough Series	1915	140.00	70.00
	X30	Girls of all Nations	1917	500.00	250.00
	50	Great War Series (New Zealand)	1916	480.00	240.00
	50	Great War Series "B" (New Zealand)	1916	480.00	240.00
	50	Great War Series "C" (New Zealand)	1916	480.00	240.00
	L1	Greeting Card ('It all depends on me')	1941	3.00	2.00
	35	Hand Shadows (Export)	1930	1080.00	540.00
	X25	Historic Grand Slams	1937	600.00	400.00
	L50	Hollandsche Oude Meesters (Dutch)	1916	1000.00	500.00
	X48	How to Recognise The Service Ranks	1930	190.00	125.00
	X150	Information Slips	1940	390.00	260.00
3798	L24	It All Depends On Me	1940	36.00	24.00
	25	Java Scenes (Export)	1932	—	—
1510	50	Life in The Services (Adhesive)	1938	52.00	32.00
	50	Life in The Services (Non-adhesive Export) A.A.	1938	75.00	50.00
	96	Modern School Atlas (Export)	1936	135.00	90.00
1085	50	National Fitness (Adhesive)	1938	36.00	24.00
357	50	National Fitness (Non-adhesive Export) A.A.	1938	54.00	36.00
	50	New Zealand Views	1928	135.00	90.00
	50	Our Empire (Export)	1936	85.00	55.00

PHOTOCARDS (Issued 1936-1939)

Ref. No.	No. in Set	Name of Set	Grade 1	Grade 2
1583	L110	Photocards A (Lancs. Football Clubs) (F)	120.00	80.00
	L110	Photocards B (N.E. Football Clubs) (F)	130.00	85.00
1585	L110	Photocards C (Yorks Football Clubs) (F)	130.00	85.00
	L165	Photocards D (Scots. Football Clubs) (F)	180.00	120.00
1587	L110	Photocards E (Midlands Football Clubs) (F)	130.00	85.00
1588	L110	Photocards F (Southern Football Clubs) (F)	115.00	75.00
28	L99	Photocards Z (General Interest Numbered 111-209) (F)	45.00	30.00
772	L11	Photocards "Supplementary" (F)	45.00	30.00
1589	L22	Photocards A Sports (F)	12.00	8.00
1590	21/22	Photocards B Coronation, Sports (F)	18.00	12.00
1591	21/22	Photocards C Personalities (Lancs) (F)	24.00	16.00

Ref. No.	No. in Set	Name of Set	Date	COMPLETE SETS Grade 1	Grade 2

ARDATH TOBACCO CO. LTD. (Cont'd)

PHOTOCARDS (Issued 1936-1939)

Ref. No.	No. in Set	Name of Set	Date	Grade 1	Grade 2
1592	L22	Photocards D Personalities (Irish) (F)		27.00	18.00
1593	L22	Photocards E Films & Sports (F)		27.00	18.00
1594	L22	Photocards F Films & Sports (F)		27.00	18.00
	L11	Photocards G Cricketers (F)		280.00	180.00

ARDATH TOBACCO CO. LTD.

Ref. No.	No. in Set	Name of Set	Date	Grade 1	Grade 2
	L66	Photocards GS Various (F)		105.00	70.00
4049	L22	Photocards H Films & Sports (F)		27.00	18.00
4050	L22	Photocards I Various (F)		36.00	24.00
	L22	Photocards J Various (F)		18.00	12.00
3934	L22	Photocards K Various (F)		27.00	18.00
3935	L44	Photocards L Various (F)		36.00	24.00
1609	45	Photocards M Various (F)		45.00	30.00
1610	L45	Photocards M Various (F) A.A.		48.00	32.00
1607	45	Photocards N Films (F)		54.00	36.00
1608	L45	Photocards N Films (F) A.A.		45.00	30.00
4052	L22	Photocards Views of the World (Group 1.) (F)		24.00	16.00
4053	L22	Photocards Views of the World (Group 2.) (F)		24.00	16.00
4020	L22	Photocards Views of the World (Group 3.) (F)		24.00	16.00
1509	25	Proverbs (1-25)	1936	32.00	16.00
2718	25	Proverbs (Export Issue 26-50)	1936	56.00	32.00
	L30	Raphael Series	1916	130.00	65.00
1611	L45	Real Photographs Group O (Film & Stage) (F)	1939	42.00	28.00
	45	Real Photos 1st Series (Film & Stage) (F)	1939	70.00	45.00
773	X18	Real Photos 1st Series (Views) (F)	1937	45.00	30.00
	54	Real Photos 2nd Series (Film & Stage) (F)	1939	75.00	50.00
774	X18	Real Photos 2nd Series (Film & Stage) (F)	1937	60.00	40.00
775	X18	Real Photos 3rd Series (Views) (F)	1937	36.00	24.00
700	X18	Real Photos 4th Series (Film & Stage) (F)	1937	60.00	40.00
776	X18	Real Photos 5th Series (Views) (F)	1938	54.00	36.00
	X18	Real Photos 6th Series (Film & Stage) (F)	1938	60.00	40.00
4040	L44	Real Photos Series 1 GP1 (Film Stars) (F)	1939	54.00	36.00
2177	L44	Real Photos Series 2 GP2 (Film Stars) (F)	1939	21.00	14.00
	L44	Real Photos Series 3 GP3 (Film Stars) (F)	1939	135.00	90.00

Ref. No.	No. in Set	Name of Set	Date	COMPLETE SETS Grade 1	Grade 2

ARDATH TOBACCO CO. LTD. (Cont'd)

Ref. No.	No. in Set	Name of Set	Date	Grade 1	Grade 2
4048	L44	Real Photos Series 3 CV3 (Views) (F)	1939	36.00	24.00
2203	L44	Real Photos Series 4 CV4 (Views) (F)	1939	16.50	10.50
4057	X36	Real Photos Series 7 (Film & Stage) (F)	1938	39.00	26.00
2478	X54	Real Photos Series 8 (Film & Stage) (F)	1938	48.00	32.00
4042	L54	Real Photos Series 9 (Film & Stage) (F)	1938	45.00	30.00
	X54	Real Photos Series 9 (Film & Stage) (F) A.A.	1938	48.00	32.00
4044	L54	Real Photos Series 10 (Film & Stage) (F)	1939	48.00	32.00
	X54	Real Photos Series 10 (Film & Stage) (F) A.A.	1939	48.00	32.00
5517	L54	Real Photos Series 11 (Film & Stage) (F)	1939	56.00	36.00
	X54	Real Photos Series 11 (Film & Stage) (F) A.A.	1939	70.00	45.00
771	L54	Real Photos Series 12 (Film & Stage) (F)	1939	48.00	32.00
1505	L54	Real Photos Series 13 (Film & Stage) (F)	1939	48.00	32.00
1506	L36	Real Photographs of Famous Landmarks (F)	1939	96.00	64.00
	X36	Real Photographs of Famous Landmarks (F) A.A.	1939	48.00	32.00
	L36	Real Photographs of Modern Aircraft (F)	1939	120.00	80.00
940	X36	Real Photographs of Modern Aircraft (F) A.A.	1939	68.00	45.00
	L30	Rembrandt Series	1916	160.00	80.00
	X30	Rembrandt Series	1916	210.00	105.00
	L40	Rembrandt Series (Back in Dutch)	1916	260.00	130.00
	L30	Rubens Series (Back in Dutch)	1916	150.00	75.00
	L30	Rubens Series (State Express Back) A.A.	1916	120.00	60.00
	L30	Rubens Series (State Express Back. N.Z.) A.A.	1916	200.00	100.00
	L30	Rubens Series (Winfred Back) A.A.	1916	200.00	100.00
	100	Scenes From Big Films (Export)	1935	280.00	140.00
	M100	Scenes From Big Films (Export) A.A.	1935	340.00	225.00
1512	50	Silver Jubilee	1935	50.00	30.00
	50	Speed Land Sea & Air (Ardath at Base Export)	1935	120.00	80.00
544	50	Speed Land Sea & Air (State Express) A.A.	1935	90.00	60.00
1952	X25	Speed Land Sea & Air (Different)	1938	36.00	24.00
	50	Sports Champions (Ardath at Base Export)	1935	90.00	60.00

A SELECTION FROM ARDATH

SET No: 1797

SET No: 544

SET No: 1086

SET No: 1300

SET No: 1512

SET No: 1514

SET No: 1513

Ref. No.	No. in Set	Name of Set	Date	COMPLETE SETS Grade 1	Grade 2
		ARDATH TOBACCO CO. LTD. (Cont'd)			
1797	50	Sports Champions (State Express) A.A.	1935	72.00	36.00
	6	Sportsmen	1953	30.00	20.00
1514	50	Stamps Rare & Interesting	1939	90.00	60.00
3931	50	Swimming Diving & Lifesaving (Export)	1937	75.00	50.00
	50	Tennis (Export)	1937	90.00	60.00
	9	The Office of Chief Whip	1955	33.00	22.00
1515	48	Trooping The Colour (Sectional)	1939	99.00	66.00
	?X12	Types of British Manhood (Circular)	1936	225.00	150.00
	X12	Types of Smokers	1929	—	—
	1	Union Jack Folder	1942	7.50	5.00
	L30	Velasquez Series	1916	160.00	80.00
	X30	Velasquez Series A.A.	1916	250.00	125.00
1086	50	Who is this? (Film Stars)	1936	140.00	70.00
	?X4	Wonderful Handcraft	1935	90.00	60.00
1300	24/25	World Views (No. 13 Not Issued)	1937	12.00	8.00
1513	50	Your Birthday Tells Your Fortune	1937	45.00	30.00
		J.A. BAILEY			
	40	Naval and Military Phrases	1900	8000.00	4000.00
		A. BAKER & CO. LTD.			
	25	Actresses, (Baker's 3 Sizes)	1900	1100.00	550.00
	L25	Actresses, (Baker's 3 Sizes)	1900	1600.00	800.00
	P?25	Actresses, (Baker's 3 Sizes)	1900	—	—
	20	Actresses, (BLARM)	1900	850.00	425.00
	10	Actresses, (HAGG)	1900	500.00	250.00
	?41	Baker's Tobacconists Shops (Back — try our 3½d Tobaccos)	1901	—	—
	41	Baker's Tobacconists Shops (Back — Cigar, Cigarette, Etc.) A.A.	1901	—	—
	25	Beauties of All Nations (Albert Baker)	1898	660.00	330.00
1684	25	Beauties of All Nations (A. Baker) A.A.	1898	400.00	200.00
	16	British Royal Family	1902	1100.00	550.00
	20	Cricketers Series	1902	10000.00	5000.00
	25	Star Girls	1898	6000.00	3000.00

Ref. No.	No. in Set	Name of Set	Date	COMPLETE SETS Grade 1	Grade 2
		J. & F. BELL LTD.			
	10	Actresses (HAGG)	1900	1300.00	650.00
	25	Beauties (Tobacco Leaf Bells's Scotia Cigs. Back)	1898	4400.00	2200.00
	25	Beauties (Tobacco Leaf Three Bell's Cigs. Back) A.A.	1899	4400.00	2200.00
	25	Colonial Series	1901	1550.00	775.00
	30	Footballers	1902	2000.00	1000.00
	60	Rigsvaabner (Arms of Countries)	1926	2400.00	1300.00
1665	25	Scottish Clan Series No. 1	1903	650.00	325.00
	60	Women of All Nations (Flag Girls)	1926	2600.00	1400.00
		R. BELLWOOD			
	18	Motor Cycle Series	1913	2900.00	1450.00
		RICHARD BENSON LTD.			
5527	L24	Old Bristol Series	1925	120.00	80.00
1543	X24	Old Bristol Series (Reprint) A.A.	1946	68.00	45.00
		BENSON & HEDGES (CANADA) LTD.			
358	48	Ancient & Modern Fire-Fighting Equipment	1947	165.00	110.00
		BENSON & HEDGES			
5635	1	Advertisement Card (Original Shop)	1973	2.50	1.25
	3	Advertisement Cards, Silk Cut	1974	4.50	2.50
	L10	B.E.A. Aircraft	1958	75.00	50.00
		HAUS BERGMANN (GERMANY)			
		FELIX BERLYN			
	25	Golfing Series	1912	—	—
	P25	Golfing Series (Postcard Back) A.A.	1912	—	—

Ref. No.	No. in Set	Name of Set	Date	COMPLETE SETS Grade 1	Grade 2
		BOCNAL TOBACCO CO.			
1279	25	Luminous Silhouettes of Beauty and Charm	1938	60.00	40.00
2179	25	Proverbs Up-to-date	1938	60.00	40.00
		ALEXANDER BOGUSLAVSKY LTD.			
	X12	Big Events on The Turf	1924	500.00	250.00
2422	25	Conan Doyle Characters (Black Back)	1923	150.00	90.00
361	25	Conan Doyle Characters (Green Back) A.A.	1923	150.00	90.00
425	25	Mythological Gods and Goddesses	1924	60.00	30.00
355	25	Sports Records (No Series Title)	1925	36.00	18.00
595	25	Sports Records 2nd Series	1925	36.00	18.00
426	25	Winners on the Turf	1925	100.00	60.00
3284	L25	Winners on the Turf A.A.	1925	190.00	95.00
		BURSTEIN ISAACS & CO.			
3892	50	Famous Prizefighters	1923	350.00	175.00
	28	London Views Series (F)	1922	135.00	90.00
		CARRERAS LTD.			
1800	24	Actresses and Their Pets (F)	1926	124.00	82.00
1231	50	A Kodak at the Zoo	1924	33.00	22.00
1232	50	A Kodak at the Zoo 2nd Series	1925	33.00	22.00
1228	48	Alice in Wonderland (round corners)	1930	80.00	40.00
825	48	Alice in Wonderland (square corners) A.A.	1930	150.00	75.00
1742	L48	Alice in Wonderland A.A.	1930	100.00	50.00
	X1	Alice in Wonderland (Instructions)	1930	14.00	8.00
1221	50	Amusing Tricks and How to Do Them	1937	36.00	24.00
	22	Battle of Waterloo	1934	30.00	20.00
	L15	Battle of Waterloo	1934	42.00	28.00
	B1	Battle of Waterloo (Instructions)	1934	9.00	6.00
2053	50	Believe It or Not	1934	36.00	24.00
401	50	Birds of The Countryside	1939	55.00	35.00
	200	Black Cat Library (Booklets)	1913	—	—
1222	50	Britain's Defences	1938	60.00	30.00

A SELECTION FROM BOGUSLAVSKY ETC.

SET No: 2179

SET No: 1684

SET No: 426

SET No: 595

SET No: 425

SET No: 2422

SET No: 355

SET No: 1953

Ref. No.	No. in Set	Name of Set	Date	COMPLETE SETS Grade 1	Grade 2
		CARRERAS LTD. (Cont'd)			
2245	25	British Costumes	1927	40.00	25.00
1881	L25	British Costumes A.A.	1927	45.00	30.00
4013	27	British Prime Ministers (F)	1928	36.00	24.00
	1	Calendar	1934	30.00	20.00
492	50	Celebrities of British History	1935	70.00	40.00
2248	25	Christie Comedy Girls (Export)	1928	56.00	36.00
3767	30	Cricketers (First Printing)	1934	110.00	70.00
3013	50	Cricketers (A Series of 50) IA	1934	190.00	120.00
16	50	Dogs and Friend	1936	15.00	10.00
208	50	Do You Know?	1939	15.00	9.00
1223	50	Famous Airmen and Airwomen	1936	85.00	45.00
1230	25	Famous Escapes	1926	50.00	30.00
2178	L25	Famous Escapes A.A.	1926	48.00	28.00
3118	P10	Famous Escapes A.A.	1926	30.00	20.00
1225	96	Famous Film Stars	1935	90.00	60.00
	6	Famous Film Stars (Six Varieties)	1935	—	—
135	48	Famous Footballers	1935	70.00	35.00
3879	25	Famous Men (Export)	1927	42.00	28.00
3799	L24	Famous Naval Men (Export) (F)	1929	42.00	28.00
	X6	Famous Posters (St. Dunstans)	1923	140.00	90.00
	L12	Famous Soldiers (Export) (F)	1928	85.00	55.00
1908	27	Famous Women (Export) (F)	1929	45.00	30.00
617	25	Figures of Fiction	1924	54.00	36.00
594	54	Film and Stage Beauties (F)	1939	28.00	18.00
1178	L54	Film and Stage Beauties (F) A.A.	1939	28.00	18.00
	L36	Film and Stage Beauties (F) A.A.	1939	28.00	18.00
2180	X36	Film and Stage Beauties (F)	1939	45.00	30.00
462	50	Film Favourites	1938	65.00	42.00
403	54	Film Stars 1st Series (F)	1937	48.00	32.00
1179	L54	Film Stars as 2nd Series (F)	1938	60.00	40.00
	X36	Film Stars Different (Export) (F)	1936	115.00	75.00
656	54	Film Stars 2nd Series (F)	1938	33.00	22.00
	X36	Film Stars 2nd Series (Export) (F)	1936	115.00	75.00
	X36	Film Stars 3rd Series (Export) (F)	1937	115.00	75.00
	X36	Film Stars 4th Series (Export) (F)	1938	115.00	75.00
265	50	Film Stars (by Desmond)	1936	60.00	36.00
2247	72	Film Stars (Oval) (F)	1934	100.00	65.00
	72	Film Stars Series (Australian issue 'Smile Away')	1933	220.00	145.00
	72	Film Stars Series (Australian issue 'Standard') A.A.	1933	150.00	100.00
	72	Film Stars Series (Titled Personalities Series Australian) A.A.	1933	150.00	100.00

A SELECTION FROM CARRERAS

SET No: 3147

SET No: 1221

SET No: 401

SET No: 1742

SET No: 2053

SET No: 2245

SET No: 1222

SET No: 1232

Ref. No.	No. in Set	Name of Set	Date	COMPLETE SETS Grade 1	Grade 2
		CARRERAS LTD. (Cont'd)			
3785	60	Flags of All Nations	Unissued	24.00	18.00
	6	Flags & Arms (Circular)	1915	650.00	325.00
	6	Flags of the Allies (Shaped All Arms)	1915	500.00	250.00
	6	Flags of the Allies (Shaped, Black Cat) A.A.	1915	500.00	250.00
	6	Flags of the Allies (Shaped, Life Ray) A.A.	1915	500.00	250.00
1226	50	Flowers	1936	26.00	16.00
1318	75	Footballers	1934	100.00	65.00
	72	Football Series (Australian issue)	1933	105.00	70.00
1280	36	Fortune Telling (Card Inset)	1926	24.00	12.00
1281	36	Fortune Telling (Head Inset)	1926	20.00	10.00
1740	L36	Fortune Telling (Card Inset)	1926	20.00	10.00
1741	L36	Fortune Telling (Head Inset)	1926	24.00	12.00
	X1	Fortune Telling (Instructions)	1926	8.50	5.50
1234	54	Glamour Girls of Stage & Films (F)	1939	28.00	18.00
2054	M54	Glamour Girls of Stage & Films (F)	1939	28.00	18.00
794	L36	Glamour Girls of Stage & Films (F)	1939	24.00	16.00
2201	X36	Glamour Girls of Stage & Films (F)	1939	30.00	20.00
1236	50	Gran-Pop	1933	21.00	14.00
1298	L50	Gran-Pop A.A.	1933	36.00	18.00
	M4	Guards Series (Military Mug Series)	1971	5.00	3.00
	M8	Guards Series (Order Up the Guards)	1970	8.00	5.00
	M16	Guards Series (Send for the Guards)	1969	12.00	8.00
1235	48	Happy Family	1925	24.00	12.00
1175	L48	Happy Family A.A.	1925	24.00	12.00
1315	25	Highwaymen	1924	80.00	40.00
495	50	History of Army Uniforms	1937	88.00	48.00
480	50	History of Naval Uniforms	1937	80.00	45.00
530	25	Horses and Hounds	1926	40.00	26.00
1166	L20	Horses and Hounds A.A.	1926	42.00	21.00
2239	P10	Horses and Hounds A.A.	1926	30.00	20.00
	4	Indian Maharajahs (300m x 280m Silks)	1930	560.00	280.00
483	50	Kings & Queens of England	1935	90.00	50.00
3733	L50	Kings & Queens of England A.A.	1935	160.00	90.00
	?L85	Lace Motifs	1916	—	—
	4	Lady with National Arms (300m x 280m)	1930	300.00	150.00
2086	27	Malayan Industries (F)	1929	10.00	6.00
	24	Malayan Scenes (F)	1928	18.00	12.00
845	L24	Malayan Scenes (F) A.A.	1928	12.00	8.00
	P7	Millionaire Competition (Folders)	1971	12.00	8.00
2094	K53	Miniature Playing Cards	1934	12.75	8.50
	4	Nature Studies (Silks size 300m x 280m)	1930	300.00	150.00

COMPLETE SETS

Ref. No.	No. in Set	Name of Set	Date	Grade 1	Grade 2
		CARRERAS LTD. (Cont'd)			
458	50	Notable M.P.'s	1929	70.00	35.00
575	M50	Notable M.P.'s A.A.	1929	40.00	22.00
3768	25	Notable Ships Past & Present (F)	1929	41.00	27.00
553	24	Old Staffordshire Figures	1926	50.00	30.00
2244	L24	Old Staffordshire Figures (Different)	1926	56.00	36.00
	P12	Old Staffordshire Figures	1926	41.00	27.00
618	24	Orchids	1925	18.00	12.00
2057	L24	Orchids A.A.	1925	18.00	12.00
1835	P24	Orchids A.A.	1925	72.00	48.00
619	50	Our Navy	1937	60.00	36.00
1260	50	Palmistry	1933	28.00	18.00
657	27	Paramount Stars (F)	1929	36.00	24.00
	24	Personality Series (Australian issue)	1933	45.00	30.00
	72	Personality Series, Film Stars (Australian issue)	1933	110.00	70.00
	72	Personality Series, Footballers (Australian issue)	1933	110.00	70.00
1319	25	Picture Puzzle Series	1923	36.00	24.00
	53	Playing Cards	1926	60.00	40.00
2929	52	Playing Cards & Dominoes (Numbered)	1929	14.00	9.00
2928	52	Playing Cards & Dominoes (Un-numbered) A.A.	1929	18.00	12.00
1544	L26	Playing Cards & Dominoes (Numbered) A.A.	1929	12.00	8.00
1545	L26	Playing Cards & Dominoes (Un-numbered) A.A.	1929	15.00	10.00
147	48	Popular Footballers	1936	45.00	30.00
1314	72	Popular Personalities (Oval) (F)	1935	84.00	48.00
	10	Popular Personalities (Oval Eire 1-10 Alternative subjects for above set)	1935	—	—
1261	25	Races Historic & Modern	1927	84.00	42.00
531	L25	Races Historic & Modern A.A.	1927	84.00	42.00
3419	P12	Races Historic & Modern	1927	84.00	42.00
1734	140	Raemeker's War Cartoons (Black Cat)	1916	230.00	115.00
	140	Raemeker's War Cartoons (Carreras) A.A.	1916	850.00	425.00
472	25	Regalia Series	1925	20.00	12.00
1176	L20	Regalia Series A.A.	1925	20.00	12.00
2181	P10	Regalia Series A.A.	1925	28.00	18.00
3831	L50	Round The World Scenic Models	1925	30.00	20.00
402	50	School Emblems	1929	42.00	26.00
3423	L40	School Emblems A.A.	1929	34.00	22.00
2182	P20	School Emblems A.A.	1929	45.00	30.00

33

Ref. No.	No. in Set	Name of Set	Date	COMPLETE SETS Grade 1	Grade 2
		CARRERAS LTD. (Cont'd)			
	L216	Sportsman's Guide — Fly Fishing (Canada)	1950	—	—
2246	48	Tapestry Reproductions of Famous Paintings (Sectional)	1928	36.00	24.00
785	52	The Greyhound Racing Game	1928	25.00	15.00
2056	L52	The Greyhound Racing Game A.A.	1928	18.00	12.00
	X1	The Greyhound Racing Game (Instructions)	1928	8.00	5.00
	B5	The Handy English-French Dictionary	1915	—	—
588	50	The Nose Game	1927	30.00	15.00
2055	L50	The Nose Game A.A.	1927	18.00	12.00
	X1	The Nose Game (Instructions)	1927	8.00	5.00
1237	50	The Science of Boxing (Black Cat)	1916	140.00	70.00
1321	50	The Science of Boxing (Carreras) A.A.	1916	260.00	130.00
369	50	Tools & How to Use Them	1925	70.00	35.00
517	80	Types of London	1919	180.00	90.00
1322	27	Views of London (F)	1929	9.00	6.00
3653	27	Views of the World (F)	1927	24.00	16.00
481	25	Wild Flower Art Series	1923	32.00	21.00
1320	50	Women on War Work	1916	520.00	260.00

CARRERAS LTD.
Post-1945 Issues

Ref. No.	No. in Set	Name of Set	Date	Grade 1	Grade 2
3137	50	British Birds	1976	4.00	—
3669	50	Flowers All the Year Round	1977	8.25	—
3800	50	Kings & Queens of England	1977	8.25	—
3031	50	Military Uniforms	1976	5.00	—
562	M8	Order up the Guards	1970	6.00	—
112	50	Palmistry	1980	45.00	—
4012	50	Sport Fish	1978	4.00	—
3165	50	Vintage Cars (With Word Filter in White Oval)	1976	6.50	—
3029	50	Vintage Cars (Without Word Filter in White Oval) A.A.	1976	5.25	—

A SELECTION FROM CARRERAS

SET No: 3137

SET No: 4012

SET No: 3165

SET No: 532

SET No: 3800

SET No: 3669

SET No: 3031

Ref. No.	No. in Set	Name of Set	Date	COMPLETE SETS Grade 1 UNCUT	Grade 2 CUT
		CARRERAS "TURF" SLIDES (Cont'd)			
2095	50	British Aircraft	1953	40.00	20.00
2412	50	British Fish	1954	20.00	10.00
1814	50	British Railway Locomotives	1952	60.00	30.00
1995	50	Celebrities of British History	1951	50.00	25.00
3138	50	Famous British Fliers	1956	80.00	40.00
1813	50	Famous Cricketers	1950	200.00	100.00
1996	50	Famous Dog Breeds	1952	48.00	24.00
532	50	Famous Film Stars	1949	72.00	36.00
835	50	Famous Footballers	1951	96.00	48.00
1815	50	Film Favourites	1948	96.00	48.00
1997	50	Film Stars	1947	90.00	45.00
836	50	Footballers	1948	100.00	50.00
2473	50	Olympics 1948	1948	100.00	50.00
1998	50	Radio Celebrities	1950	60.00	30.00
1999	50	Sports	1949	80.00	40.00
2000	50	Zoo Animals	1954	16.00	8.00
		CARRERAS AND MARCIANUS			
	1	Photo Miniatures Folder	1909	130.00	65.00
	100	War Series	1916	—	—
		CARRICK & CO.			
	12	Military Terms	1901	1250.00	625.00
		P. J. CARROLL & CO.			
31	25	Birds	1939	26.00	16.00
	25	British Naval Series	1915	1450.00	725.00
	25	County Louth G.R.A. Team & Officials	1913	—	—
	25	Derby Winners (Black back)	1915	3200.00	1600.00
	25	Derby Winners (Green back) A.A.	1915	3200.00	1600.00
	24	Jig Saw Puzzles	1935	500.00	250.00
	25	Ship Series	1937	190.00	125.00

Ref. No.	No. in Set	Name of Set	Date	COMPLETE SETS Grade 1	Grade 2
		THE CASKET TOBACCO & CIGARETTES CO. LTD.			
	?2	Cricket Fixture cards	1905	1020.00	510.00
	1	Cyclists Lighting Up Table	1909	400.00	200.00
	?11	Football Fixture Cards	1909	—	—
	?2	Road Maps	1909	760.00	380.00
		CASTELANO BROS. LTD. (INDIA)			
	52	Beauties, Playing Card Inset	1898	2000.00	1000.00
		S. CAVANDER & CO.			
	?25	Beauties (PLUMS)	1898	6000.00	3000.00
		CAVANDERS LTD.			
1077	25	Ancient Chinese	1926	48.00	24.00
96	25	Ancient Egypt	1928	40.00	20.00
1752	L25	Ancient Egypt (Different)	1928	44.00	22.00
1523	36	Animal Studies (F)	1936	18.00	12.00
1524	50	Beauty Spots of Great Britain (F)	1927	12.00	8.00
1753	M50	Beauty Spots of Great Britain (F) A.A.	1927	12.00	8.00
1075	54	Camera Studies (F)	1926	12.00	8.00
1169	M56	Camera Studies (F) I.A.	1926	12.00	8.00
797	30	Cinema Stars	1934	45.00	30.00
2914	M50	Coloured Stereoscopic (ST)	1931	21.00	14.00
1565	25	Feathered Friends	1926	60.00	40.00
1076	25	Foreign Birds A.A.	1926	40.00	24.00
2915	M50	Glorious Britain (ST)	1930	23.00	15.00
3671	25	Little Friends	1924	27.00	18.00
1074	72	Peeps into Many Lands 1st Series (ST)	1927	24.00	16.00
3717	M72	Peeps into Many Lands 1st Series (ST) A.A.	1927	24.00	16.00
2241	X36	Peeps into Many Lands 1st Series (ST) A.A.	1927	75.00	50.00
1073	72	Peeps into Many Lands 2nd Series (ST)	1928	24.00	16.00
3718	M72	Peeps into Many Lands 2nd Series (ST) A.A.	1928	24.00	16.00
590	48	Peeps into Many Lands 3rd Series (ST)	1929	18.00	12.00
3719	M48	Peeps into Many Lands 3rd Series (ST) A.A.	1929	18.00	12.00

Ref. No.	No. in Set	Name of Set	Date	COMPLETE SETS Grade 1	Grade 2
		CAVANDERS LTD. (Cont'd)			
3720	M48	Peeps into Many Lands 3rd (Reprinted) (ST) A.A.	1929	18.00	12.00
589	48	Peeps into Prehistoric Times 4th Series (ST)	1930	24.00	16.00
3721	M48	Peeps into Prehistoric Times 4th Series (ST) A.A.	1930	24.00	16.00
	33	Photographs (F)	1924	60.00	40.00
	L48	Regimental Standards	1923	600.00	400.00
1525	25	Reproduction of Celebrated Oil Paintings	1925	36.00	24.00
1526	108	River Valleys (F)	1926	39.00	26.00
1173	M108	River Valleys (F) A.A.	1926	48.00	32.00
119	25	School Badges	1928	21.00	14.00
1170	M30	The Colonial Series (F)	1925	15.00	10.00
1424	54	The Homeland Series (Black back) (F)	1924	22.50	15.00
1423	50	The Homeland Series (Blue back) (F) I.A.	1924	39.00	26.00
1172	M50	The Homeland Series (F) I.A.	1924	14.00	9.00
1171	M56	The Homeland Series (F) I.A.	1924	18.00	12.00
1743	M25	The Nation's Treasures	1925	18.00	12.00
1174	M30	Wordsworth's Country (F)	1926	21.00	14.00
		W. A. & A. C. CHURCHMAN			
	25	Actresses (Unicoloured)	1898	2600.00	1300.00
	26	Actresses (FROGA A)	1901	1300.00	650.00
	26	Actresses (FROGA B)	1901	1600.00	800.00
1180	M48	Air Raid Precautions	1938	18.00	12.00
	M48	Air Raid Precautions (Overseas No. I.T.C. Clause) A.A.	1938	75.00	50.00
1654	25	Army Badges of Rank	1916	180.00	90.00
171	50	Association Footballers 1st Series	1938	40.00	20.00
201	50	Association Footballers 2nd Series	1939	48.00	24.00
	50	A Tour Round The World	1911	500.00	250.00
	1	Australia Cricket Fixture Booklet	1899	—	—
	12	Beauties (CERF)	1899	1060.00	530.00
	25	Beauties (CHOAB)	1901	5000.00	2500.00
	M25	Beauties (CHOAB) (Circular)	1900	—	—
	25	Beauties (FECKSA)	1903	3600.00	1800.00
	25	Beauties (GRACC)	1899	3200.00	1600.00

SET No: 3279

SET No: 2670

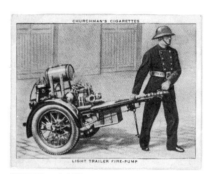

SET No: 1180

SET No: 3476

SET No: 270

SET No: 1654

SET No: 1683

**COMPLETE
SETS**

Ref. No.	No. in Set	Name of Set	Date	Grade 1	Grade 2
		W. A. & A. C. CHURCHMAN (Cont'd)			
1574	50	Birds & Eggs	1906	520.00	260.00
	20	Boer War Cartoons	1901	3400.00	1700.00
	20	Boer War Generals (CLAM Black front)	1901	1300.00	650.00
	20	Boer War Generals (CLAM Brown front) A.A.	1901	1300.00	650.00
1511	25	Boxing	1922	160.00	80.00
270	50	Boxing Personalities	1938	200.00	100.00
2264	50	Boy Scouts 1st Series	1916	460.00	230.00
3363	50	Boy Scouts 2nd Series	1916	460.00	230.00
1683	50	Boy Scouts 3rd Series (Blue Back)	1916	800.00	400.00
1682	50	Boy Scouts 3rd Series (Brown Back) A.A.	1916	460.00	230.00
3649	25	British Film Stars	1934	65.00	40.00
1462	55	Can You Beat Bogey at St. Andrews?	1934	170.00	110.00
1463	55	Can You Beat Bogey at St. Andrews? (Red Overprint) A.A.	1934	170.00	110.00
1461	25	Cathedrals & Churches	1924	60.00	40.00
1028	X12	Cathedrals & Churches A.A.	1924	150.00	100.00
1458	50	Celebrated Gateways	1925	140.00	90.00
	41	Celebrities & Actresses Boer War Period	1901	—	—
1024	M1	Christmas Greeting Card	1938	2.50	1.50
1456	25	Civic Insignia and Plate	1926	60.00	40.00
1457	50	Contract Bridge	1935	30.00	20.00
169	50	Cricketers	1936	260.00	140.00
1460	25	Curious Dwellings	1926	60.00	40.00
3361	L12	Curious Dwellings A.A.	1925	75.00	50.00
1459	25	Curious Signs	1925	60.00	40.00
2266	38	Dogs and Fowls	1908	360.00	180.00
537	25	Eastern Proverbs 1st Series	1931	28.00	16.00
548	L12	Eastern Proverbs 1st Series A.A.	1931	48.00	32.00
1069	25	Eastern Proverbs 2nd Series	1932	28.00	16.00
2183	L12	Eastern Proverbs 2nd Series A.A.	1933	21.00	14.00
2135	L12	Eastern proverbs 3rd Series	1933	12.00	8.00
2136	L12	Eastern Proverbs 4th Series	1934	12.00	8.00
549	50	East Suffolk Churches (Black)	1912	160.00	80.00
1464	50	East Suffolk Churches (Sepia) A.A.	1917	160.00	80.00
1443	50	Empire Railways	1931	190.00	95.00
2262	25	Famous Cricket Colours	1928	120.00	70.00
1466	50	Famous Golfers	1927	520.00	260.00
143	L12	Famous Golfers 1st Series A.A.	1927	320.00	160.00
144	L12	Famous Golfers 2nd Series	1928	320.00	160.00
486	25	Famous Railway Trains	1929	100.00	60.00
145	L12	Famous Railway Trains 1st Series A.A.	1928	95.00	55.00

Ref. No.	No. in Set	Name of Set	Date	COMPLETE SETS Grade 1	Grade 2

W. A. & A. C. CHURCHMAN (Cont'd)

Ref. No.	No. in Set	Name of Set	Date	Grade 1	Grade 2
3789	L12	Famous Railway Trains 2nd Series	1929	95.00	55.00
3382	50	Fish & Bait	1914	450.00	225.00
1070	50	Fishes of the World	1912	520.00	260.00
2267	50	Flags & Funnels of Leading Steamship Lines	1912	550.00	275.00
	50	Football Club Colours	1909	700.00	350.00
5588	50	Footballers (Brown)	1906	2000.00	1000.00
	50	Footballers (Action Pictures & Inset)	1914	850.00	425.00
1465	52	Frisky	1925	100.00	60.00
478	50	History & Development of the British Empire	1934	75.00	50.00
313	M48	Holidays in Britain (Views & Maps)	1937	12.75	8.50
	M48	Holidays in Britain (Views & Maps No. I.T.C. Clause) A.A.	1937	75.00	50.00
314	M48	Holidays in Britain (Views only)	1938	12.75	8.50
	M48	Holidays in Britain (Views only No. I.T.C. Clause) A.A.	1938	75.00	50.00
	40	Home & Colonial Regiments	1902	2800.00	1400.00
123	40	Howlers	1937	12.00	8.00
1181	L16	Howlers A.A.	1936	12.00	8.00
	50	Interesting Buildings	1905	500.00	250.00
1409	25	Interesting Door Knockers	1928	70.00	45.00
1573	25	Interesting Experiments	1929	50.00	30.00
202	50	In Town Tonight	1938	14.00	8.00
5502	L12	Italian Art Exhibition 1st Series	1930	25.00	12.50
3032	L12	Italian Art Exhibition 2nd Series	1931	25.00	12.50
203	50	Kings of Speed	1939	60.00	30.00
1444	50	Landmarks in Railway Progress	1931	180.00	110.00
2343	L12	Landmarks in Railway Progress 1st Series A.A.	1932	80.00	50.00
3652	L12	Landmarks in Railway Progress 2nd Series	1932	80.00	50.00
3770	50	Lawn Tennis	1928	130.00	85.00
334	L12	Lawn Tennis A.A.	1928	95.00	65.00
525	50	Legends of Britain	1936	70.00	40.00
1885	L12	Legends of Britain A.A.	1936	36.00	18.00
404	25	Life in a Liner	1930	40.00	26.00
551	L12	Life in a Liner A.A.	1930	36.00	24.00
	50	Medals	1910	450.00	225.00
2263	50	Men of the Moment in Sport	1928	180.00	90.00
554	L12	Men of the Moment in Sport 1st Series A.A.	1929	130.00	65.00

Ref. No.	No. in Set	Name of Set	Date	COMPLETE SETS Grade 1	Grade 2
		W. A. & A. C. CHURCHMAN (Cont'd)			
555	L12	Men of the Moment in Sport 2nd Series	1929	130.00	65.00
1185	M48	Modern Wonders	1938	21.00	14.00
	M48	Modern Wonders (No. I.T.C. Clause) A.A.	1938	120.00	60.00
2261	25	Musical Instruments	1924	85.00	55.00
	1	Mystery Wording Revolving Card	1907	—	—
405	25	Nature's Architects	1930	40.00	26.00
556	L12	Nature's Architects A.A.	1930	40.00	26.00
	L&X55	Olympic Winners Through the Years (Cartoon Design)	1956	84.00	42.00
	50	Phil May Sketches (Churchman's Cigarettes)	1912	650.00	325.00
	50	Phil May Sketches (Gold Flake) A.A.	1912	550.00	275.00
	M48	Pioneers	(Unissued)	—	—
1072	25	Pipes of the World	1927	90.00	55.00
1445	50	Prominent Golfers	1931	620.00	310.00
126	L12	Prominent Golfers A.A.	1931	360.00	180.00
3034	50	Racing Greyhounds	1934	170.00	85.00
1468	25	Railway Working 1st Series	1926	130.00	65.00
3274	L12	Railway Working 1st Series A.A.	1926	160.00	80.00
3769	25	Railway Working 2nd Series	1927	110.00	55.00
3275	L13	Railway Working 2nd Series A.A.	1927	170.00	85.00
1789	L12	Railway Working 3rd Series	1927	160.00	80.00
3305	50	Regimental Colours & Cap Badges	1912	500.00	250.00
1469	50	Rivers & Broads	1921	440.00	220.00
3894	50	Rivers & Broads of Norfolk & Suffolk A.A.	1922	360.00	180.00
170	50	Rugby Internationals	1935	120.00	60.00
2268	50	Sectional Cycling Map	1913	480.00	240.00
1915	50	Silhouettes of Warships	1915	640.00	320.00
1446	50	Sporting Celebrities	1931	180.00	90.00
1470	25	Sporting Trophies	1927	60.00	40.00
3276	L12	Sporting Trophies A.A.	1927	75.00	50.00
1471	25	Sports & Games in Many Lands	1929	70.00	40.00
406	25	The Houses of Parliament & Their Story	1931	72.00	42.00
479	25	The Inns of Court	1922	100.00	60.00
200	50	The King's Coronation	1937	16.00	10.00
2137	L15	The King's Coronation A.A.	1937	18.00	12.00
1183	M48	The Navy at Work	1937	14.00	8.00
	M48	The Navy at Work (No. I.T.C. Clause) A.A.	1937	100.00	50.00
496	50	The Queen Mary	1936	100.00	60.00
2144	L16	The Queen Mary A.A.	1936	80.00	50.00
1184	M48	The RAF at Work	1938	64.00	36.00

A SELECTION FROM CHURCHMAN

SET No: 203

SET No: 525

SET No: 2263

SET No: 1915

SET No: 2894

SET No: 1184

SET No: 3770

SET No: 2343

Ref. No.	No. in Set	Name of Set	Date	COMPLETE SETS Grade 1	Grade 2
		W. A. & A. C. CHURCHMAN (Cont'd)			
	M48	The RAF at Work			
		(No. I.32T.C. Clause) A.A.	1937	85.00	55.00
452	50	The Story of London	1930	100.00	60.00
1182	L12	The Story of London A.A.	1930	48.00	32.00
20	50	The Story of Navigation	1937	15.50	9.50
2073	L12	The Story of Navigation A.A.	1935	21.00	14.00
	D40	The World of Sport (Cartoon Design)	1961	48.00	32.00
1475	36	3 Jovial Golfers in Search of the Perfect Course	1934	160.00	90.00
	72	3 Jovial Golfers (Irish Issue, green over-printing)	1934	440.00	280.00
124	50	Treasure Trove	1937	12.50	7.50
2074	L12	Treasure Trove A.A.	1935	22.00	14.00
	25	Types of British & Colonial Troops	1899	1900.00	950.00
542	25	Warriors of All Nations	1929	100.00	60.00
2243	L12	Warriors of All Nations 1st Series A.A.	1929	80.00	45.00
2334	L12	Warriors of All Nations 2nd Series	1931	80.00	45.00
488	50	Well Known Ties 1st Series	1934	60.00	35.00
2184	L12	Well Known Ties 1st Series A.A.	1934	35.00	20.00
489	50	Well Known Ties 2nd Series	1934	48.00	28.00
2185	L12	Well Known Ties 2nd Series A.A.	1935	35.00	20.00
1472	25	Wembley Exhibition	1924	70.00	45.00
1473	50	West Suffolk Churches	1919	130.00	65.00
	50	Wild Animals of the World	1907	500.00	250.00
1186	M48	Wings Over the Empire	1939	18.00	12.00
	M48	Wings Over the Empire (No. I.T.C. Clause) A.A.	1939	60.00	40.00
122	50	Wonderful Railway Travel	1937	20.00	12.00
2240	L12	Wonderful Railway Travel A.A.	1937	20.00	12.00
3425	50	World's Wonders Old & New	(Unissued)	25.00	15.00

CIGARETTE COMPANY
(Jersey Channel Isles)

	72	Jersey Footballers	1911	560.00	280.00

A SELECTION FROM CHURCHMAN & CLARKE

SET No: 542

SET No: 452

SET No: 5644

SET No: 124

SET No: 122

SET No: 20

SET No: 684

SET No: 4141

Ref. No.	No. in Set	Name of Set	Date	COMPLETE SETS Grade 1	Grade 2
		WM. CLARKE & SON			
2283	25	Army Life	1915	460.00	230.00
	16	Boer War Celebrities	1901	650.00	325.00
684	50	Butterflies and Moths	1912	640.00	320.00
	30	Cricketer Series	1901	6000.00	3000.00
	66	Football Series	1902	1600.00	800.00
	14	Cricket Terms) Total of	1900	1000.00	500.00
	12	Cycling Terms) 50 Sporting	1900	800.00	400.00
	12	Football Terms) Terms	1900	800.00	400.00
	12	Golf Terms)	1900	1800.00	900.00
4141	25	Marine Series	1907	520.00	260.00
1000	50	Royal Mail	1914	760.00	380.00
	20	Tobacco Leaf Girls	1898	13000.00	6500.00
5644	25	Well Known Sayings	1900	950.00	475.00
		HENRY CLAY AND BOCK & CO. (CUBA)			
		J. H. CLURE & SON			
	30	Army Pictures, Cartoons, etc.	1916	3800.00	1900.00
	50	War Portraits	1916	5600.00	2800.00
		J. LOMAX COCKAYNE			
	50	War Portraits	1916	5600.00	2800.00
		COHEN WEENEN & CO.			
	40	Actresses, Footballers & Jockeys (F)	1901	3000.00	1500.00
	26	Actresses (FROGA)	1900	2700.00	1350.00
	24	Beauties (BOCCA)	1899	3200.00	1600.00
	25	Beauties (GRACC)	1899	3800.00	1900.00
3225	65	Celebrities (Black & White 250 back)	1906	500.00	250.00
	25	Celebrities (Black & White 500 back) A.A.	1906	500.00	250.00
	45	Celebrities, Coloured (100 back)	1901	300.00	150.00
	45	Celebrities, Coloured (Plain back) A.A.	1901	—	—

Ref. No.	No. in Set	Name of Set	Date	COMPLETE SETS Grade 1	Grade 2
		COHEN WEENEN & CO. (Cont'd)			
	121	Celebrities (coloured 250 back)			
		1-451.A.	1901	1200.00	600.00
	39	Celebrities, Gainsborough (250 back)	1902	2500.00	1250.00
	B39	Celebrities, Gainsborough (Calendar back) A.A.	1902	—	—
	B39	Celebrities, Gainsborough (Plain back) A.A.	1902	—	—
	B30	Celebrities, Gainsborough (400 back) A.A.	1902	550.00	275.00
	M172	Celebrities, Gainsborough II (F)	1901	—	—
2484	25	Cricketers	1926	375.00	225.00
	20	Cricketers, Footballers & Jockeys	1900	650.00	325.00
1395	25	Famous Boxers (Black back)	1912	430.00	215.00
	25	Famous Boxers (Green back) A.A.	1912	420.00	210.00
	40	Fiscal Phrases	1902	600.00	300.00
2594	60	Football Captains	1907	1100.00	550.00
	100	Heroes of Sport	1898	7000.00	3500.00
1426	40	Home & Colonial Regiments (100 back)	1901	500.00	250.00
	40	Home & Colonial Regiments (250 back) A.A.	1901	700.00	350.00
3227	20	Interesting Buildings & Views	1902	280.00	140.00
	K53	Miniature Playing Cards	1902	340.00	170.00
3228	20	Nations (Blue back)	1902	420.00	210.00
	20	Nations (Plain back) A.A.	1902	—	—
552	20	Nations (Descriptive) A.A.	1923	160.00	80.00
	40	Naval and Military Phrases (Blue back)	1904	2000.00	1000.00
	40	Naval and Military Phrases (Red back) A.A.	1905	1200.00	600.00
3005	50	Owners, Jockeys, Footballers, Cricketers (Series No. 2)	1906	800.00	400.00
	20	Owners, Jockeys, Footballers, Cricketers (Series No. 3)	1907	360.00	180.00
895	30	Proverbs	1902	760.00	380.00
705	20	Russo Japanese War Series	1903	500.00	250.00
	25	Silhouettes of Celebrities	1903	480.00	240.00
3007	50	Star Artistes (Series No. 4)	1907	920.00	460.00
	L16	Victoria Cross Heroes (Silk)	1915	1050.00	525.00
1733	50	V.C. Heroes (Numbered 51-100)	1916	660.00	330.00
	25	V.C. Heroes (51-75 Anonymous) A.A.	1916	500.00	250.00
3230	50	War Series	1916	640.00	320.00
3223	30	Wonders of the World (Series No. 6)	1908	360.00	180.00
1384	30	Wonders of the World (re-issued with gilt border) A.A.	1923	160.00	80.00

Ref. No.	No. in Set	Name of Set	Date	COMPLETE SETS Grade 1	Grade 2
		CO-OPERATIVE WHOLESALE SOCIETY (C.W.S.)			
	5	Advertisement Cards	1915	1900.00	950.00
621	24	African Types	1936	10.50	6.50
849	M50	Beauty Spots of Great Britain	1936	14.00	9.00
622	50	Boy Scout Badges	1939	40.00	26.00
702	25	Boy Scout Series	1912	1100.00	550.00
2186	48	British and Foreign Birds	1938	40.00	25.00
	50	British Sports Series	1904	2500.00	1250.00
5271	25	Cooking Recipes	1923	75.00	50.00
703	29	Co-operative Buildings & Works	1909	550.00	275.00
5515	24	English Roses	1924	110.00	70.00
2277	48	Famous Bridges	1937	27.00	18.00
2277a	50	Famous Bridges + 2 extra cards I.A.	1937	42.00	28.00
447	48	Famous Buildings	1935	36.00	24.00
558	25	How To Do It	1924	70.00	45.00
3278	48	Musical Instruments	1934	220.00	140.00
685	25	Parrot Series	1910	1300.00	650.00
5272	48	Poultry	1927	255.00	170.00
2278	48	Railway Engines	1936	180.00	120.00
2279	24	Sailing Craft	1935	42.00	28.00
	18	War Series	1914	700.00	350.00
3301	48	Wayside Flowers (Brown Back)	1923	115.00	75.00
2085	48	Wayside Flowers (Grey Back)	1928	30.00	20.00
623	48	Wayside Woodland Trees	1924	150.00	100.00
2009	24	Western Stars	1957	7.50	5.00
		COOPER & CO's STORES LTD.			
	25	Boer War Celebrities — STEW (Alphaure, Mixture' back)	1902	4800.00	2400.00
	25	Boer War Celebrities — STEW (Gladys Cigars back) A.A.	1902	4800.00	2400.00
		COPE BROS. & CO. LTD.			
	20	Actresses (BLARM Design back)	1901	1250.00	625.00
	20	Actresses (BLARM Plain back) A.A.	1901	1250.00	625.00
	6	Actresses (COPEIS)	1901	1250.00	625.00
	26	Actresses (FROGA)	1899	4000.00	2000.00
	50	Actresses & Beauties (F)	1900	1000.00	500.00
	52	Beauties (P/C) (Inset)	1900	4000.00	2000.00

A SELECTION FROM C. W. S. & COPE

SET No: 685

SET No: 2278

SET No: 447

SET No: 3639

SET No: 1396

SET No: 558

SET No: 3408

SET No: 5272

SET No: 1666

Ref. No.	No. in Set	Name of Set	Date	COMPLETE SETS Grade 1	Grade 2
		COPE BROS. & CO. LTD. (Cont'd)			
	15	Beauties (PAC)	1899	1850.00	925.00
	25	Beauties & Actors	1903	—	—
2821	50	Boats of the World	1912	920.00	460.00
1396	25	Boxers (1-25)	1914	320.00	160.00
5406	25	Boxers (26-50)	1914	320.00	160.00
5407	25	Boxers (51-75)	1914	320.00	160.00
	25	Boxers (76-100)	1914	550.00	275.00
1557	25	Boxers (101-125) (Army Boxers)	1914	380.00	190.00
3232	1	Boxers (New World Champion)	1915	60.00	30.00
2187	25	Boxing Lessons	1935	75.00	50.00
3677	35	Boy Scouts and Girl Guides	1910	580.00	290.00
	X25	Bridge Problems (Folders)	1925	920.00	460.00
	25	British Admirals	1915	440.00	220.00
1666	50	British Warriors	1912	800.00	400.00
635	25	Castles	1939	24.00	16.00
1962	25	Cathedrals	1939	30.00	20.00
3639	50	Characters from Scott	1905	850.00	425.00
	50	Characters from Scott (Narrow Card) A.A.	1905	650.00	325.00
704	115	Chinese Series	1903	—	—
3640	50	Cope's Golfers	1904	4800.00	2400.00
	50	Cope's Golfers (Narrow Card) A.A.	1904	4000.00	2000.00
277	L25	Dickens Characters Series	1939	25.00	15.00
3111	50	Dickens Gallery	1910	760.00	380.00
	B50	Dickens Gallery (Cope's Solace back) A.A.	1909	—	—
3675	50	Dogs of the World	1912	620.00	310.00
3408	25	Eminent British Regiments	1908	430.00	215.00
	24	Flags, Arms & Types of All Nations	1904	300.00	150.00
	30	Flags of Nations (Bond of Union Back)	1903	—	—
	30	Flags of Nations (Plain back) A.A.	1903	480.00	240.00
	B50	General Knowledge	1925	260.00	130.00
546	32	Golf Strokes	1923	345.00	230.00
5472	60	Happy Families	1937	90.00	60.00
3722	M50	Household Hints	1925	100.00	65.00
	X20	Kenilworth Phrases	1910	—	—
3306	30	Lawn Tennis Strokes	1924	100.00	65.00
	L50	Modern Dancing (Folders)	1926	—	—
1536	50	Music Hall Artistes (Series of 50)	1913	2800.00	1400.00
	50	Music Hall Artistes (No Series of 50) A.A.	1913	800.00	400.00
	472	Noted Footballers (Clips Cigarettes)	1911	—	—
	195	Noted Footballers (Solace Cigarettes)	1911	—	—

A SELECTION FROM COPE ETC.

SET No: 3307

SET No: 3673

SET No: 1536

SET No: 3722

SET No: 3616

SET No: 3306

SET No: 1962

SET No: 2287

Ref. No.	No. in Set	Name of Set	Date	Grade 1	Grade 2
		COPE BROS. & CO. LTD. (Cont'd)			
	24	Occupations for Women	1898	3000.00	1500.00
	X12	Photo Albums for the Million (Buff)	1902	280.00	140.00
	X12	Photo Albums for the Million (Green) (DIFF)	1902	280.00	140.00
2419	25	Pigeons	1926	150.00	100.00
	52	Playing Cards (Rulers as Court Cards. Round corners)	1900	1050.00	525.00
	52	Playing Cards (Rulers as Court Cards. Square corners) A.A.	1900	1050.00	525.00
	30	Scandinavian Actors & Actresses	1910	2300.00	1150.00
3676	50	Shakespeare Gallery	1906	820.00	410.00
	50	Shakespeare Gallery (Narrow Card) A.A.	1906	750.00	375.00
2287	25	Song Birds	1926	100.00	65.00
560	25	Sports & Pastimes	1925	110.00	70.00
379	L25	The Game of Poker	1936	10.50	7.00
3307	25	The World's Police	1937	90.00	60.00
27	L25	Toy Models — A Country Fair	1925	10.50	7.00
	25	Uniforms of Soldiers and Sailors (Circular Medallion back)	1898	1220.00	610.00
	25	Uniforms of Soldiers and Sailors (Circular Medallion back Narrow Card) A.A.	1898	1120.00	560.00
	25	Uniforms of Soldiers and Sailors (Square Medallion back) A.A.	1898	1800.00	900.00
	25	Uniforms of Soldiers and Sailors (Square Medallion back Narrow Card) A.A.	1898	1000.00	500.00
3673	50	V.C. & D.S.O. Naval & Flying Heroes (Un-numbered)	1916	640.00	320.00
	25	V.C. & D.S.O. Naval & Flying Heroes (51-75)	1916	320.00	160.00
	20	War Pictures	1915	310.00	155.00
	50	War Series (Leaders & Warships)	1915	950.00	475.00
	25	Wild Animals & Birds	1907	720.00	360.00
		E. CORONEL			
	25	Types of British and Colonial Troops	1900	2600.00	1300.00

Ref. No.	No. in Set	Name of Set	Date	COMPLETE SETS Grade 1	Grade 2
		W. T. DAVIES & SONS			
	?50	Actresses (DIVAN)	1903	6200.00	3100.00
2785	30	Aristocrats of the Turf (1-30)	1924	110.00	70.00
	12	Aristocrats of the Turf (31-42)	1924	190.00	125.00
3219	36	Aristocrats of the Turf 2nd Series	1924	120.00	80.00
706	25	Army Life	1915	440.00	220.00
	12	Beauties	1902	800.00	400.00
3290	25	Boxing	1924	130.00	65.00
	50	Flags & Funnels of Leading Steamship Lines	1913	850.00	425.00
	?10	Newport Football Club	1904	2400.00	1200.00
	?5	Royal Welsh Fusiliers	1904	1600.00	800.00
		S. H. DAWES			
	30	Army Pictures, Cartoons, etc.	1916	3700.00	1850.00
		J. W. DEWHURST			
	30	Army Pictures, Cartoons, etc.	1916	3700.00	1850.00
		R. J. DEXTER			
1451	30	Borough Arms	1900	36.00	18.00
		GEORGE DOBIE & SON LTD.			
	L25	Bridge Problems (Folders)	1933	—	—
561	M32	Four Square Books (1-32)	1963	36.00	24.00
5599	M32	Four Square Books (33-64)	1963	11.00	7.00
5600	M32	Four Square Books (65-96)	1963	11.00	7.00
2814	25	Weapons of All Ages	1924	230.00	130.00
		DOMINION TOBACCO CO. (1929) LTD.			
1794	25	Old Ships 1st Series	1934	42.00	28.00
2043	25	Old Ships 2nd Series	1935	21.00	14.00
428	25	Old Ships 3rd Series	1936	21.00	14.00
2281	25	Old Ships 4th Series	1936	30.00	20.00

Ref. No.	No. in Set	Name of Set	Date	COMPLETE SETS Grade 1	Grade 2
		MAJOR DRAPKIN & CO.			
	12	Actresses (Plain backs)	1910	130.00	65.00
	1	Advertisement Card (The Greys)	1935	5.00	2.50
	8	Advertisement Cards	1929	60.00	40.00
	?X1	Army Insignia	1916	250.00	125.00
	50	Around Britain (Export)	1929	75.00	50.00
	L50	Around Britain (Export) A.A.	1926	150.00	100.00
	50	Around the Mediterranean (Export)	1926	75.00	50.00
	L50	Around the Mediterranean (Export) A.A.	1926	150.00	100.00
362	40	Australian & English Test Cricketers (F) (Export)	1928	90.00	60.00
	?100	Bandmaster Conundrums	1907	800.00	400.00
5265	25	British Beauties (Export)	1930	75.00	50.00
2750	36	Celebrities of the Great War (F)	1916	40.00	20.00
	34	Celebrities of the Great War A.A. (Plain back) (F)	1916	36.00	18.00
	B96	Cinematograph Actors	1913	1200.00	600.00
2415	15	Dogs and their Treatment	1924	150.00	100.00
2238	L15	Dogs and their Treatment A.A.	1924	100.00	66.00
	50	Girls of Many Lands	1929	140.00	90.00
2188	M50	Girls of Many Lands A.A.	1929	24.00	14.00
3297	25	"How to Keep Fit" (Crayel Cigarettes)	1912	440.00	220.00
	25	"How to Keep Fit" (Drapkin's Cigarettes) A.A.	1912	440.00	220.00
	25	"How to Keep Fit" (Drapkin's Cigarettes officially cut) A.A.	1912	400.00	200.00
2189	54	Life at Whipsnade Zoo (F)	1934	36.00	22.00
2138	50	Limericks	1929	54.00	36.00
2335	36	National Types of Beauty (F)	1928	30.00	20.00
1939	25	Optical Illusions	1926	72.00	48.00
3467	L25	Optical Illusions A.A.	1926	90.00	60.00
3308	25	Palmistry	1927	72.00	48.00
1401	L25	Palmistry A.A.	1926	80.00	50.00
	48	Photogravure Masterpieces	1915	500.00	250.00
3813	25	Puzzle Pictures	1926	90.00	60.00
1991	L25	Puzzle Pictures A.A.	1926	105.00	70.00
	M40	Regimental Colours & Badges of the Indian Army (Silk)	1915	260.00	130.00
	P25	Soldiers & Their Uniforms (Crayol Cigarettes. Cut-outs)	1914	120.00	60.00
	P25	Soldiers & Their Uniforms (Drapkin's Cigarettes. Cut-outs) A.A.	1914	120.00	60.00
565	P22/25	Soldiers & Their Uniforms (Cut-outs) A.A.	1914	36.00	18.00

A SELECTION OF SETS ON DOGS

GALLAHER SET 2075

SET 1887

GODFREY PHILLIPS SET 243

SET 1996

GALLAHER SET 442

GALLAHER SET 592

SET 368

SET 2194

Ref. No.	No. in Set	Name of Set	Date	COMPLETE SETS Grade 1	Grade 2
		MAJOR DRAPKIN & CO. (Cont'd)			
707	35/36	Sporting Celebrities in Action (F) (Export)	1930	60.00	40.00
1935	40	The Game of Sporting Snap	1928	110.00	70.00
		The Game of Sporting Snap Instruction Booklet	1928	6.00	4.00
566	12	Views of the World (Plain backs)	1915	80.00	40.00
	6	Warships	1911	104.00	52.00
		J. DUNCAN & CO. LTD.			
1442	50	Evolution of the Steamship	1925	78.00	48.00
1442a	47/50	Evolution of the Steamship (less three cards) A.A.	1925	36.00	24.00
	48	Flags, Arms and Types of Nations	1912	2400.00	1200.00
	20	Inventors & Their Inventions	1915	1600.00	800.00
2851	30	Scottish Clans, Arms of Chiefs and Tartans (Black back)	1912	3600.00	1800.00
	30	Scottish Clans, Arms of Chiefs and Tartans (Green back) A.A.	1912	950.00	475.00
	L72	Scottish Gems 1st Series (Coloured)	1912	1400.00	700.00
	L50	Scottish Gems 2nd Series (Coloured)	1913	1200.00	600.00
	L50	Scottish Gems 3rd Series (Coloured)	1914	1200.00	600.00
3878	L50	Scottish Gems (Not Coloured)	1925	30.00	20.00
	25	Types of British Soldiers	1910	2000.00	1000.00
		EDWARDS, RINGER & BIGG			
567	25	Abbeys and Castles (Stag back)	1912	320.00	160.00
	25	Abbeys & Castles (Statue of Liberty back) A.A.	1912	320.00	160.00
	25	Abbeys & Castles (Typeset back) A.A.	1912	400.00	200.00
2893	25	Alpine Views (Stag Design back)	1912	320.00	160.00
	25	Alpine Views (Statue of Liberty back) A.A.	1912	320.00	160.00
	50	A Tour Round the World	1909	800.00	400.00
3906	12	Beauties (CERF)	1905	1100.00	550.00
	25	Beauties (FECKSA)	1900	1600.00	800.00

A SELECTION FROM MAJOR DRAPKIN ETC.

SET No: 1991

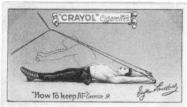

SET No: 3297

SET No: 2138

SET No: 1442

SET No: 362

SET No: 1935

SET No: 5265

**COMPLETE
SETS**

Ref. No.	No. in Set	Name of Set	Date	Grade 1	Grade 2
		EDWARDS, RINGER & BIGG (Cont'd)			
	50	Birds and Their Eggs	1906	1020.00	510.00
	25	Boer War Celebrities	1901	1800.00	900.00
	?25	Boer War & Boxer Rebellion Sketches	1901	4400.00	2200.00
569	25	British Trees and Their Uses	1935	85.00	55.00
	1	Calendar & Lighting up Table	1899	500.00	250.00
	1	Calendar (Exmoor Hunt back)	1905	380.00	190.00
	1	Calendar	1910	480.00	240.00
571	50	Celebrated Bridges	1924	160.00	90.00
2041	50	Cinema Stars	1923	80.00	50.00
2042	L25	Cinema Stars	1923	70.00	40.00
	25	Coast & Country (Stag Design back)	1911	320.00	160.00
	25	Coast & Country (Statue of Liberty back) A.A.	1911	320.00	160.00
2937	23	Dogs Series (Exmoor Hunt back)	1908	340.00	170.00
	23	Dogs Series (Klondyke back) A.A.	1908	150.00	75.00
	28	Dominoes	1912	—	—
	3	Easter Manoeuvers of our Volunteers	1897	1000.00	500.00
3939	37	Flags of All Nations (Horizontal, Globe & Flags back)	1907	380.00	190.00
880	37	Flags of All Nations (Horizontal, Exmoor Hunt back) A.A.	1907	420.00	210.00
	37	Flags of All Nations (Horizontal, Stag Design back) A.A.	1907	380.00	190.00
	37	Flags of All Nations (Vertical back) A.A.	1907	380.00	190.00
3322	25	Garden Life	1934	100.00	65.00
879	25	How to tell Fortunes	1929	140.00	80.00
3889	50	Life on Board a Man of War	1905	850.00	425.00
	1	Miners Bound for Klondyke	1897	700.00	350.00
1894	50	Mining	1925	150.00	100.00
3303	25	Musical Instruments	1924	120.00	70.00
572	25	Optical Illusions	1936	75.00	50.00
1413	25	Our Pets	1926	75.00	50.00
1631	25	Our Pets, 2nd Series	1926	85.00	55.00
573	25	Past & Present	1928	120.00	80.00
578	10	Portraits of H.M. (King Edward VII) in Uniform	1902	760.00	380.00
429	25	Prehistoric Animals	1924	140.00	80.00
	X1	Ringer's Racing Guide (Folder)	1957	—	—
5541	25	Sports & Games in Many Lands	1935	130.00	80.00
	56	War Map of the Western Front	1916	950.00	475.00
1852	54	War Map of the Western Front (Series 2) (Exmoor Hunt back)	1917	900.00	450.00
	54	War Map of the Western Front (Series 2) (New York Mixture back) A.A.	1917	900.00	450.00

A SELECTION FROM EDWARDS RINGER ETC.

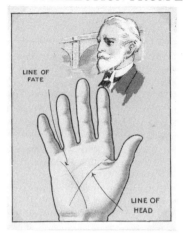

SET No: 1401

SET No: 2042

SET No: 578

SET No: 3303

SET No: 429

SET No: 1413

SET No: 3906

**COMPLETE
SETS**

Ref. No.	No. in Set	Name of Set	Date	Grade 1	Grade 2
		W. & F. FAULKNER			
	26	Actresses (FROGA)	1900	2000.00	1000.00
583	25	Angling	1929	170.00	110.00
	12	'Ation Series	1901	450.00	225.00
	25	Beauties (Coloured)	1898	2600.00	1300.00
	50	Beauties (FECKSA)	1901	1550.00	775.00
	16	British Royal Family	1901	920.00	460.00
	1	Calendar	1924	—	—
3426	50	Celebrated Bridges	1925	150.00	100.00
584	12	Coster Series	1900	450.00	225.00
	20	Cricketers Series	1901	7200.00	3600.00
	12	Cricket Terms	1899	1120.00	560.00
5324	12	Football Terms 1st Series	1900	450.00	225.00
5540	12	Football Terms 2nd Series	1900	450.00	225.00
	12	Golf Terms	1901	1400.00	700.00
	12	Grenadier Guards	1899	500.00	250.00
	40	Kings & Queens	1902	1600.00	800.00
4163	12	Kipling Series	1900	500.00	250.00
2349	12	Military Terms 1st Series	1899	400.00	200.00
585	12	Military Terms 2nd Series	1899	400.00	200.00
908	12	Nautical Terms 1st Series	1900	430.00	215.00
3220	12	Nautical Terms 2nd Series (Grenadier Cigarettes)	1900	420.00	210.00
	12	Nautical Terms 2nd Series (Union Jack Cigarettes) A.A.	1900	450.00	225.00
2190	25	Old Sporting Prints	1930	90.00	60.00
503	25	Optical Illusions	1935	75.00	50.00
687	90	Our Colonial Troops	1900	2000.00	1000.00
3218	20	Our Gallant Grenadiers	1902	600.00	300.00
688	40	Our Gallant Grenadiers (with I.T.C. Clause) I.A.	1903	1650.00	825.00
3723	25	Our Pets	1926	100.00	65.00
5220	25	Our Pets, 2nd Series	1926	85.00	55.00
5222	12	Policemen of the World	1899	720.00	360.00
5410	12	Police Terms	1899	450.00	225.00
485	25	Prominent Racehorses, of the Present Day	1923	120.00	60.00
5526	25	Prominent Racehorses, of the Present Day, 2nd Series	1924	180.00	90.00
	12	Puzzle Series (Grenadier Cigarettes)	1898	1400.00	700.00
	12	Puzzle Series (Nosegay Cigarettes) A.A.	1898	1100.00	550.00
686	25	South African War Series	1901	520.00	260.00
	12	Sporting Terms	1900	550.00	275.00
3221	12	Street Cries	1902	500.00	250.00

Ref. No.	No. in Set	Name of Set	Date	COMPLETE SETS Grade 1	Grade 2
		W. & F. FAULKNER (Cont'd)			
5223	12	The Language of Flowers (Grenadier Cigarettes)	1900	700.00	350.00
	12	The Language of Flowers (Nosegay Cigarettes) A.A.	1900	700.00	350.00
		FRANKLYN DAVEY & CO.			
5567	12	Beauties (CERF)	1905	1300.00	650.00
	50	Birds	1895	4200.00	2100.00
	10	Boer War Generals	1901	1600.00	800.00
2078	25	Boxing	1924	110.00	55.00
1614	25	Ceremonial & Court Dress	1915	370.00	185.00
1628	50	Children of All Nations (Cut-outs)	1934	40.00	25.00
	1	Comic Dog Folder (6 parts, 183mm x 65mm when open)	1930	—	—
3362	50	Football Club Colours	1909	900.00	450.00
587	50	Historic Events	1924	200.00	100.00
1627	25	Hunting	1925	40.00	20.00
	50	Modern Dance Steps, 1st Series	1929	255.00	170.00
841	50	Modern Dance Steps, 2nd Series	1931	45.00	25.00
3341	50	Naval Dress & Badges	1916	840.00	420.00
	50	Overseas Dominions (Australia)	1923	320.00	160.00
	25	Star Girls	1901	6000.00	3000.00
	10	Types of Smokers	1898	920.00	460.00
	50	Wild Animals of the World	1902	800.00	400.00
		GALLAHER LTD.			
	?111	Actors & Actresses	1901	850.00	425.00
1001	48	Aeroplanes	1939	58.00	36.00
1439	25	Aesops Fables (Series of 25)	1931	44.00	24.00
449	25	Aesops Fables (Series of 50) A.A.	1931	44.00	24.00
1002	100	Animals & Birds of Commercial Value	1921	90.00	45.00
271	48	Army Badges	1939	40.00	25.00
2076	L24	Art Treasures of the World	1930	15.00	10.00
1006	100	Association Football Club Colours	1910	750.00	375.00
1783	52	Beauties (with Playing Card Inset)	1905	1050.00	525.00

Ref. No.	No. in Set	Name of Set	Date	COMPLETE SETS Grade 1	Grade 2

GALLAHER LTD. (Cont'd)

Ref. No.	No. in Set	Name of Set	Date	Grade 1	Grade 2
	52	Beauties (without Playing Card Inset) A.A.	1905	1050.00	525.00
758	M48	Beautiful Scotland (F)	1939	36.00	24.00
	50	Birds & Eggs	1905	650.00	325.00
1434	100	Birds Nests & Eggs	1919	210.00	105.00
1554	100	Boy Scout Series (Green back, Belfast & London)	1911	280.00	140.00
	86/100	Boy Scout Series (Green back, London & Belfast) A.A.	1911	280.00	140.00
1004	100	Boy Scout Series (Brown back) A.A.	1922	165.00	110.00
642	48	British Birds	1937	17.00	11.00
1005	100	British Birds by Rankin (by George Rankin)	1923	110.00	60.00
	100	British Birds by Rankin (by Rankin) A.A.	1923	—	—
2942	75	British Champions of 1923	1924	110.00	70.00
1777	50	British Naval Series	1914	320.00	160.00
591	48	Butterflies & Moths	1938	16.00	10.00
1030	25	Champion Animals & Birds of 1923	1924	36.00	24.00
17	48	Champions (No Name on front)	1934	21.00	14.00
450	48	Champions (With Name re-drawn) A.A.	1934	21.00	14.00
514	48	Champions 2nd Series	1935	18.00	12.00
1003	48	Champions of Screen & Stage (Red back)	1934	40.00	24.00
597	48	Champions of Screen & Stage (Blue back, Gallaher's Cigarettes) A.A.	1934	60.00	40.00
759	48	Champions of Screen & Stage (Blue back, Gallaher Ltd.) A.A.	1934	60.00	40.00
1432	100	Cinema Stars	1926	180.00	110.00
	M48	Coastwise (F)	1938	30.00	20.00
2075	24	Dogs (Caption in block)	1934	20.00	12.00
	24	Dogs (Caption in script) A.A.	1934	—	—
611	L24	Dogs (Caption in block) A.A.	1934	20.00	12.00
	L24	Dogs (Caption in script) A.A.	1934	—	—
442	48	Dogs 1st Series	1936	30.00	19.00
592	48	Dogs 2nd Series	1938	27.00	16.00
	100	English & Scotch Views (F)	1910	320.00	160.00
1431	100	Fables & Their Morals (Numbered in name panel)	1912	240.00	120.00
	100	Fables & Their Morals (Thick numerals) A.A.	1922	100.00	50.00
437	100	Fables & Their Morals (Thin numerals) A.A.	1922	120.00	60.00
1799	100	Famous Cricketers	1926	380.00	190.00

A SELECTION FROM FAULKNER ETC.

SET No: 583

SET No: 686

SET No: 3426

SET No: 5220

SET No: 2190

SET No: 687

SET No: 688

SET No: 4163

**COMPLETE
SETS**

Ref. No.	No. in Set	Name of Set	Date	Grade 1	Grade 2
		GALLAHER LTD. (Cont'd)			
470	48	Famous Film Scenes	1935	50.00	30.00
1011	50	Famous Footballers (Brown back)	1926	140.00	70.00
1008	100	Famous Footballers (Green back)	1925	220.00	110.00
95	48	Famous Jockeys	1936	60.00	35.00
468	48	Film Episodes	1936	50.00	30.00
1009	48	Film Partners	1935	50.00	30.00
	M24	Flags (Silk)	1915	280.00	140.00
	M48	Flying (F)	1938	48.00	32.00
1744	50	Footballers (Red back, 1-50)	1928	130.00	65.00
465	50	Footballers (Red back, 51-100)	1928	150.00	75.00
1745	50	Footballers in Action	1928	140.00	70.00
612	48	Garden Flowers	1938	12.00	8.00
	100	How To Do It	1916	440.00	220.00
	100	Interesting Views (Black & White) (F)	1923	120.00	80.00
	100	Interesting Views (Coloured) (F) A.A.	1924	225.00	150.00
	200	Irish Views Scenery (Numbered 1-200) (F)	1910	360.00	180.00
	200	Irish Views Scenery (Numbered 201-400) (F)	1910	360.00	180.00
	200	Irish Views Scenery (Un-numbered) (F) A.A.	1910	240.00	120.00
	200	Irish Views Scenery (Numbered 401-600) (F)	1910	400.00	200.00
	L48	Island Sporting Celebrities (F)	1938	45.00	30.00
	100	Kute Kiddies	1916	500.00	250.00
	50	Latest Actresses (Black & White) (F)	1909	1000.00	500.00
	50	Latest Actresses (Chocolate brown) (F) A.A.	1909	1300.00	650.00
494	50	Lawn Tennis Celebrities	1928	220.00	120.00
3235	24	Motor Cars	1934	130.00	75.00
385	48	My Favourite Part	1939	50.00	30.00
	M48	Our Countryside (F)	1938	36.00	24.00
371	100	Plants of Commercial Value	1917	120.00	60.00
613	48	Portraits of Famous Stars	1935	70.00	40.00
513	48	Racing Scenes	1938	40.00	25.00
1020	50	Regimental Colours & Standards	1912	520.00	260.00
1021	100	Robinson Crusoe	1928	240.00	130.00
1380	50	Royalty Series	1902	550.00	275.00
2077	L48	Scenes from the Empire (F)	1939	18.00	11.00
	48	Screen Lovers (Summit)	Unissued	—	—
1014	48	Shots from Famous Films	1935	40.00	25.00
	M24	Shots from the Films (F)	1936	90.00	60.00
497	48	Signed Portraits of Famous Stars	1935	120.00	70.00
272	48	Sporting Personalities	1936	26.00	16.00

SET No: 5567

SET No: 841

SET No: 2078

SET No: 1627

SET No: 271

SET No: 1777

SET No: 1628

SET No: 611

Ref. No.	No. in Set	Name of Set	Date	**COMPLETE SETS** Grade 1	Grade 2
		GALLAHER LTD. (Cont'd)			
1015	100	Sports Series	1912	700.00	350.00
	100	Stage & Variety Celebrities (Collotype Gallaher back)	1899	—	—
	100	Stage & Variety Celebrities (Collotype Gallaher back) A.A.	1899	—	—
35	48	Stars of Screen & Stage (Brown back)	1935	90.00	60.00
643	48	Stars of Screen & Stage (Green back) A.A.	1935	50.00	30.00
2936	25	The Allies Flags	1914	200.00	100.00
1732	100	The Great War Series	1915	380.00	190.00
1731	100	The Great War Series	1915	420.00	210.00
2164	25	The Great War Series V.C. Heroes 1st	1915	180.00	90.00
1676	25	The Great War Series V.C. Heroes 2nd	1915	170.00	85.00
1677	25	The Great War Series V.C. Heroes 3rd	1915	170.00	85.00
1678	25	The Great War Series V.C. Heroes 4th	1916	170.00	85.00
1840	25	The Great War Series V.C. Heroes 5th	1916	170.00	85.00
1679	25	The Great War Series V.C. Heroes 6th	1917	170.00	85.00
1980	25	The Great War Series V.C. Heroes 7th	1917	170.00	85.00
2751	25	The Great War Series V.C. Heroes 8th	1918	170.00	85.00
	48	The Navy (Gallaher back)	1937	35.00	20.00
1017	48	The Navy (Park Drive back) A.A.	1937	24.00	16.00
372	100	The Reason Why	1924	96.00	48.00
3672	111	The South African Series	1901	1100.00	550.00
1436	100	The Zoo Aquarium	1924	130.00	80.00
273	48	Trains of the World	1937	45.00	30.00
1022	100	Tricks & Puzzles Series (Green back)	1913	620.00	310.00
1438	100	Tricks & Puzzles Series (Black back) (DIFF)	1933	130.00	65.00
1955	50	Types of the British Army (Battle Honours back)	1898	800.00	400.00
3000	50	Types of the British Army (Three Pipes, Brown back) A.A.	1898	680.00	340.00
891	50	Types of the British Army (Three Pipes, Green back) A.A.	1898	680.00	340.00
	50	Types of the British Army (Now in Three, Brown back) A.A.	1898	680.00	340.00
1930	50	Types of the British Army (51-100 The Three Pipes, Brown back)	1900	680.00	340.00
	50	Types of the British Army (51-100 Now in Three, Brown back) A.A.	1900	680.00	340.00
1023	100	Useful Hints Series	1915	450.00	225.00
	25	Views in Northern Ireland	1912	1450.00	725.00
1435	50	Votaries of the Weed	1916	500.00	250.00

A SELECTION OF GARDENING SETS

SET 261

SET 264

SET 262

SET 61

SET 263

SET 649

SET 3

SET 67

SET 204

Details of Grading on Page 5.

Ref. No.	No. in Set	Name of Set	Date	COMPLETE SETS Grade 1	Grade 2
		GALLAHER LTD. (Cont'd)			
	100	Why Is It? (Brown back)	1915	450.00	225.00
	100	Why Is It? (Green back) A.A.	1915	420.00	210.00
593	48	Wild Animals	1937	15.00	10.00
644	48	Wild Flowers	1939	15.75	10.50
1019	100	Woodland Trees Series	1912	560.00	280.00
1437	50	Zoo Tropical Birds 1st Series	1928	85.00	50.00
614	50	Zoo Tropical Birds 2nd Series	1929	85.00	50.00
		GASPA			
	?20	Our Great Novelists	1931	1400.00	700.00
		SAMUEL GAWITH			
	X25	The English Lakeland	1923	570.00	380.00
		GENERAL CIGAR COMPANY, (CANADA)			
	X36	Northern Birds	1968	48.00	32.00
		F. GENNARI LTD.			
	50	War Portraits	1916	5500.00	2750.00
		LOUIS GERARD LTD.			
972	50	Modern Armaments (Numbered)	1938	30.00	20.00
973	50	Modern Armaments (Un-numbered) A.A.	1938	45.00	30.00
	24	Screen Favourites (back — Louis Gerard & Company)	1937	90.00	60.00
	24	Screen Favourites (back — Louis Gerard, Limited) A.A.	1937	90.00	60.00
	48	Screen Favourites & Dancers	1937	120.00	80.00

A SELECTION FROM GALLAHER LTD.

SET No: 95

SET No: 1540

SET No: 1009

SET No: 1745

SET No: 612

SET No: 1020

SET No: 371

SET No: 385

Ref. No.	No. in Set	Name of Set	Date	**COMPLETE SETS** Grade 1	Grade 2
		HIGNETT BROS. & CO.			
2062	50	Actors Natural & Character Studies	1938	80.00	40.00
	26	Actresses (FROGA)	1900	2300.00	1150.00
	25	Actresses Photogravure	1900	1020.00	510.00
	28	Actresses (PILPI I)	1901	920.00	460.00
	50	Actresses (PILPI II) (F)	1901	1000.00	500.00
	1	Advertisement Card Smoking Mixture	1900	—	—
3411	50	A.F.C. Nicknames	1933	320.00	160.00
1482	50	Air Raid Precautions	1939	42.00	28.00
	60	Animal Pictures	1899	2900.00	1450.00
564	50	Arms & Armour	1924	200.00	125.00
	25	Beauties (CHOAB)	1900	4800.00	2400.00
	50	Beauties — (Gravure 'Cavalier' back)	1898	5200.00	2600.00
	50	Beauties — (Gravure 'Golden Butterfly' back) A.A.	1898	5200.00	2600.00
	B50	Beauties (Chess Cigarettes) (F)	1927	63.00	42.00
	B50	Beauties (No brand name) (F)	1927	75.00	50.00
598	50	British Birds & Their Eggs	1938	115.00	75.00
599	50	Broadcasting	1935	140.00	90.00
	16	Cabinet 1900	1900	1900.00	950.00
2291	25	Cathedrals & Churches	1909	160.00	80.00
2897	50	Celebrated Old Inns	1925	180.00	120.00
1922	50	Champions of 1936	1937	140.00	90.00
3905	25	Common Objects of the Sea-Shore	1924	75.00	50.00
1484	25	Company Drill	1915	150.00	75.00
	50	Coronation Procession	1937	125.00	85.00
430	50	Dogs	1936	130.00	70.00
3874	50	Football Caricatures	1935	140.00	90.00
5497	50	Football Club Captains	1935	140.00	90.00
318	25	Greetings of the World	1907	120.00	60.00
3904	25	Historical London	1926	85.00	55.00
2061	50	How to Swim	1935	45.00	30.00
3004	50	Interesting Buildings	1905	440.00	220.00
1483	25	International Caps & Badges	1924	110.00	70.00
3142	25	Life in Pond & Stream	1925	85.00	55.00
	40	Medals (Butterfly Cigarettes)	1900	1500.00	750.00
	40	Medals (above officially cut off) A.A.	1900	1500.00	750.00
	25	Military Portraits	1914	190.00	95.00
	50	Modern Railways	1936	140.00	90.00
3489	25	Modern Statesmen (Butterfly Cigarettes back)	1906	250.00	125.00
	25	Modern Statesmen (Pioneer Cigarettes back) A.A.	1906	250.00	125.00
	20	Music Hall Artistes	1898	1800.00	900.00

A SELECTION FROM GALLAHER

SET No: 3672

SET No: 1955

SET No: 3000

SET No: 273

SET No: 1017

SET No: 1980

SET No: 1778

SET No: 1435

COMPLETE SETS

Ref. No.	No. in Set	Name of Set	Date	Grade 1	Grade 2
		HIGNETT BROS. & CO. (Cont'd)			
1486	50	Ocean Greyhounds	1938	100.00	60.00
2292	25	Panama Canal	1914	260.00	130.00
	12	Pretty Girl Series "RASH"	1900	1070.00	535.00
5498	50	Prominent Cricketers of 1938	1938	165.00	110.00
600	50	Prominent Racehorses of 1933	1934	140.00	90.00
463	50	Sea Adventure	1939	24.00	16.00
3140	25	Ships, Flags & Cap Badges 1st Series	1926	100.00	65.00
1485	25	Ships, Flags & Cap Badges 2nd Series	1927	115.00	75.00
602	50	Shots from the Films	1936	130.00	80.00
373	25	The Prince of Wales Empire Tour	1924	78.00	52.00
	1	The Regulated Animated Butterfly (Shaped)	1910	—	—
	50	Trick Billiards	1934	165.00	110.00
3304	25	Turnpikes	1927	85.00	55.00
	25	V.C. Heroes	1901	1950.00	975.00
	20	Yachts (back — Black on White)	1898	2000.00	1000.00
	20	Yachts (back — Gold on Black) A.A.	1898	2200.00	1100.00
1920	50	Zoo Studies	1937	60.00	40.00
		R. & J. HILL LTD.			
	25	Actresses (Belle of New York Series)	1899	900.00	450.00
	20	Actresses (chocolate tinted Hill's Tobacco back)	1917	640.00	320.00
	20	Actresses (chocolate tined Issued with Hill's back) A.A.	1917	640.00	320.00
	20	Actresses (chocolate tinted Plain back) A.A.	1917	640.00	320.00
	30	Actresses, Continental ('Black and White Whiskey' back)	1905	900.00	450.00
	30	Actresses, Continental (Plain back) A.A.	1905	850.00	425.00
	30	Actresses, Continental ('The Seven Wonders' back) A.A.	1905	850.00	425.00
	26	Actresses (FROGA A)	1900	2200.00	1100.00
	25	Actresses (HAGG Hill's High Class)	1900	1600.00	800.00
	25	Actresses (HAGG Smoke Hill's Stockrider) A.A.	1900	1650.00	825.00
603	20	Animal Series (Crowfoot Cigarettes back)	1909	820.00	410.00
	20	Animal Series (Hill's back) A.A.	1909	920.00	460.00
	20	Animal Series (Plain back) A.A.	1909	820.00	410.00

A SELECTION FROM HIGNETT & HILL

SET No: 463

SET No: 3304

SET No: 3489

SET No: 2497

SET No: 1920

SET No: 2191

SET No: 605

SET No: 2147

COMPLETE SETS

Ref. No.	No. in Set	Name of Set	Date	Grade 1	Grade 2
		R. & J. HILL LTD. (Cont'd)			
2191	25	Aviation Series (Gold Flake back)	1934	80.00	50.00
	25	Aviation Series (R. & J. Hill back) A.A.	1934	66.00	44.00
	?15	Battleships (Pipe Smoke Oceanic back)	1909	3500.00	1750.00
	?15	Battleships (Plain back) A.A.	1909	900.00	450.00
605	25	Battleships & Crests	1900	640.00	320.00
	12	Boer War Generals	1901	750.00	375.00
	20	Breeds of Dogs (Archer's back)	1915	640.00	320.00
	20	Breeds of Dogs (Badminton back)	1915	640.00	320.00
	20	Breeds of Dogs (Verbena Mixture back) A.A.	1915	640.00	320.00
	20	Breeds of Dogs (Spinet Tobacco back) A.A.	1915	640.00	320.00
606	L30	Britain's Stately Homes (Silk)	1916	200.00	100.00
	?50	British Navy Series	1902	1900.00	950.00
5345	L40	Canvas Masterpieces Series 1 (Silk)	1917	110.00	55.00
	L40	Canvas Masterpieces Series 2 (Silk)	1917	150.00	75.00
	X10	Canvas Masterpieces Series 2 (Silk)	1917	50.00	25.00
1821	50	Caricatures of Famous Cricketers	1926	150.00	100.00
1821b	L50	Caricatures of Famous Cricketers A.A.	1926	90.00	60.00
2147	50	Celebrities of Sport (Gold Flake back)	1939	105.00	70.00
	50	Celebrities of Sport (R. & J. Hill back) A.A.	1939	75.00	50.00
	P5	Chinese Pottery & Porcelain (Silk)	1915	20.00	10.00
	X11	Chinese Pottery & Porcelain Series 2 (Silk)	1915	100.00	50.00
474	35	Cinema Celebrities (These Cigarettes are — back)	1936	27.00	18.00
	35	Cinema Celebrities (The Spinet House — back) A.A.	1936	27.00	18.00
875	50	Colonial Troops (Sweet American back)	1901	1900.00	950.00
	30	Colonial Troops (Hill's Leading Lines back) A.A.	1901	1600.00	800.00
	30	Colonial Troops (Perfection vide Dress back) A.A.	1901	1600.00	800.00
2497	40	Crystal Palace Souvenir Cards	1937	55.00	35.00
2327	48	Decorations & Medals (Gold Flake back)	1940	150.00	100.00
	48	Decorations & Medals (R. & J. Hill back) A.A.	1940	90.00	60.00
	48	Famous Cinema Celebrities Set 1 (Spinet back) (F)	1931	200.00	130.00

A SELECTION FROM R. & J. HILL

SET No: 501

SET No: 439

SET No: 3429

SET No: 3731

SET No: 1250

SET No: 344

SET No: 668

Ref. No.	No. in Set	Name of Set	Date	COMPLETE SETS Grade 1	Grade 2
		R. & J. HILL LTD. (Cont'd)			
	48	Famous Cinema Celebrities Set 1 (without Spinet back) (F) A.A.	1931	200.00	130.00
	L48	Famous Cinema Celebrities Set 2 (Series A) (F) A.A.	1931	240.00	160.00
	50	Famous Cinema Celebrities Set 2 (Series C Devon back) (F)	1932	375.00	250.00
	50	Famous Cinema Celebrities Set 2 (Series C Toucan back) (F) A.A.	1932	375.00	250.00
	M50	Famous Cinema Celebrities Set 2 (Series D Kadi back) (F) A.A.	1932	210.00	140.00
	M50	Famous Cinema Celebrities Set 2 (Series D without Kadi back) (F) A.A.	1932	210.00	140.00
	28	Famous Cricketers Series (Blue back)	1912	2500.00	1250.00
	28	Famous Cricketers Series (Red back) A.A.	1912	2500.00	1250.00
1990	40	Famous Cricketers	1923	250.00	150.00
3484	50	Famous Cricketers, including S. Africa Test Team	1924	250.00	150.00
	L50	Famous Cricketers, including S. Africa Test Team A.A.	1924	275.00	165.00
	50	Famous Dog Breeds (Airmail Cigs.)	1954	300.00	200.00
	L30	Famous Engraving Series II	1910	230.00	115.00
2170	40	Famous Film Stars	1938	48.00	32.00
5523	40	Famous Film Stars (Arabic Text) A.A.	1938	54.00	36.00
	20	Famous Football Series	1912	440.00	220.00
5343	50	Famous Footballers (Brown)	1923	160.00	90.00
3902	50	Famous Footballers (Proprietors of Hy. Archer back)	1939	100.00	65.00
469	50	Famous Footballers (Shoreditch address back) A.A.	1939	90.00	60.00
4147	25	Famous Footballers (51-75)	1939	72.00	48.00
2430	25	Famous Pictures (Hill Fine Art Cigarette back)	1913	160.00	80.00
	25	Famous Pictures (Hill Cigarette Series) A.A.	1913	160.00	80.00
	50	Famous Ships (matt front)	1939	50.00	30.00
431	50	Famous Ships (varnished front) A.A.	1940	50.00	30.00
2333	48	Film Stars & Celebrity Dancers	1935	100.00	65.00
	30	Flags & Flags with Soldiers	1901	1200.00	600.00
	24	Flags, Arms & Types of Nations	1910	440.00	220.00
	20	Football Captains Series (Numbered 41-60)	1906	720.00	360.00

Ref. No.	No. in Set	Name of Set	Date	COMPLETE SETS Grade 1	Grade 2
		R. & J. HILL LTD. (Cont'd)			
2749	20	Fragments from France (Coloured)	1916	760.00	380.00
609	10	Fragments from France (Sepia)	1916	500.00	250.00
610	10	Fragments from France (Black & White)	1916	1200.00	600.00
713	L23	Great War Leaders Series 10 (Silk)	1916	220.00	110.00
515	50	Historic Places from Dickens Classics	1926	45.00	30.00
2778	L50	Historic Places from Dickens Classics A.A.	1925	45.00	30.00
3485	50	Holiday Resorts	1925	36.00	24.00
2729	L50	Holiday Resorts A.A.	1925	42.00	28.00
1672	20	Inventors & Their Inventions	1907	140.00	70.00
636	20	Inventors & Their Inventions (Plain back)	1934	27.00	18.00
637	20	Inventors & Their Inventions (21-40)	1907	230.00	115.00
	15	Japanese Series (Black & White)	1905	850.00	425.00
	15	Japanese Series (Coloured) A.A.	1905	1200.00	600.00
	30	Lighthouse Series (framelines on front)	1903	1600.00	800.00
	20	Lighthouse Series (no framelines on front) A.A.	1903	1250.00	625.00
638	50	Magical Puzzles	1937	72.00	48.00
1795	50	Modern Beauties	1939	58.00	38.00
473	30	Music Hall Celebrities ‑ ‑ Past & Present	1930	75.00	50.00
2667	L30	Music Hall Celebrities — Past & Present A.A.	1930	75.00	50.00
4092	20	National Flag Series	1914	220.00	110.00
1979	30	Nature Pictures	1930	36.00	24.00
3619	30	Nautical Songs	1937	27.00	18.00
	B?20	Naval Series (Un-numbered)	1902	1400.00	700.00
	30	Naval Series (Numbered)	1902	600.00	300.00
315	30	Our Empire Series	1929	10.50	7.00
3727	L30	Our Empire Series A.A.	1929	12.50	7.50
639	M30	Popular Footballers Series A	1935	80.00	50.00
2351	M20	Popular Footballers Series B	1935	60.00	40.00
	20	Prince of Wales Series	1911	400.00	200.00
	L?15	Prints from Noted Pictures	1908	2400.00	1200.00
3728	50	Public Schools & Colleges	1923	39.00	26.00
2918	L50	Public Schools & Colleges A.A.	1923	39.00	26.00
3483	75	Public Schools & Colleges I.A.	1923	75.00	50.00
640	L75	Public Schools & Colleges A.A.	1923	80.00	55.00
2139	50	Puzzle Series	1937	45.00	30.00
	42	Real Photographs Set 1 (Bathing Belles)	1930	120.00	80.00

Ref. No.	No. in Set	Name of Set	Date	COMPLETE SETS Grade 1	Grade 2
		R. & J. HILL LTD. (Cont'd)			
	42	Real Photographs Set 2 (Beauties) (F)	1930	115.00	75.00
	20	Rhymes	1904	850.00	425.00
	50	Scenes from the Films (F)	1934	150.00	100.00
508	40	Scenes from the Films	1938	30.00	20.00
641	35	Scientific Inventions & Discoveries (Black & Yellow)	1929	44.00	26.00
501	35	Scientific Inventions & Discoveries (Coloured) A.A.	1929	44.00	26.00
667	L35	Scientific Inventions & Discoveries (Coloured) A.A.	1929	44.00	26.00
	50	Sports (Numbered front & back) (F)	1934	210.00	140.00
	50	Sports Series (Numbered on front) (F) A.A.	1934	330.00	220.00
	50	Sports (Untitled, numbered front only) (F) A.A.	1934	415.00	275.00
	28	Statuary Set 1	1908	400.00	200.00
668	30	Statuary Set 2	1909	300.00	150.00
	25	Statuary Set 3	1910	600.00	300.00
3277	30	The All Blacks	1924	150.00	100.00
439	50	The Railway Centenary 1st Series	1924	120.00	60.00
3157	L50	The Railway Centenary 1st Series A.A.	1925	120.00	60.00
1250	25	The Railway Centenary 2nd Series	1925	80.00	40.00
3900	L25	The Railway Centenary 2nd Series A.A.	1925	80.00	40.00
2275	25	The River Thames 1-25	1924	52.00	32.00
2276	25	The River Thames 26-50	1924	42.00	26.00
669	L50	The River Thames A.A.	1924	66.00	44.00
	100	Transfers	1935	375.00	250.00
	20	Types of the British Army (Badminton back)	1914	1000.00	500.00
	20	Types of the British Army (Verbena back) A.A.	1914	1000.00	500.00
341	L48	Views of Interest 1st Series (Spinet, House back) (F)	1938	18.00	12.00
475	L48	Views of Interest 1st Series (Sunripe back) (F) A.A.	1938	15.00	10.00
342	L48	Views of Interest 2nd Series (F)	1938	15.00	10.00
343	L48	Views of Interest 3rd Series (F)	1939	15.00	10.00
344	L48	Views of Interest 4th Series (F)	1939	26.00	15.00
1168	L48	Views of Interest 5th Series (F)	1939	26.00	15.00
1167	L48	Views of Interest — Canada (F)	1940	24.00	14.00
	L48	Views of Interest — India (F)	1940	165.00	110.00

Ref. No.	No. in Set	Name of Set	Date	COMPLETE SETS Grade 1	Grade 2
		R. & J. HILL LTD. (Cont'd)			
1251	50	Views of London	1925	54.00	36.00
3730	L50	Views of London A.A.	1925	60.00	40.00
670	L50	Views of the River Thames	1924	69.00	46.00
671	25	War Series	1915	460.00	230.00
3731	50	Who's Who in British Films	1927	75.00	50.00
4015	L50	Who's Who in British Films A.A.	1927	75.00	50.00
3233	84	Wireless Telephony	1923	120.00	80.00
1661	L20	Wireless Telephony Broadcasting Series	1923	68.00	45.00
3429	25	World's Masterpieces 2nd Series	1914	72.00	48.00
3732	50	Zoological Series	1924	45.00	30.00
2917	L50	Zoological Series A.A.	1924	53.00	35.00
		HUDDEN & CO.			
	26	Actresses (FROGA)	1900	2500.00	1250.00
	25	Beauties (CHOAB)	1900	2250.00	1125.00
	?25	Beauties (Crown Seal)	1899	5000.00	2500.00
	24	Beauties (HUMPS) (Blue, scroll back)	1899	2800.00	1400.00
	24	Beauties (HUMPS) (Orange, scroll back) A.A.	1899	2500.00	1250.00
	24	Beauties (HUMPS) (typeset back) A.A.	1899	5500.00	2750.00
	?12	Comic Phrases	1900	2200.00	1100.00
	25	Famous Boxers	1927	1300.00	650.00
	25	Flags of All Nations	1903	760.00	380.00
	18	Pretty Girl Series	1900	2400.00	1200.00
	50	Public Schools & Colleges	1924	130.00	85.00
	25	Soldiers of the Century (Nd. 26-50)	1903	2000.00	1000.00
	25	Sports & Pastimes	1926	2600.00	1300.00
	25	Star Girls	1900	3200.00	1600.00
	48	The Japanese Flower Game	1899	7500.00	3750.00
	25	Types of Smokers	1902	1900.00	950.00
		JAMES ILLINGWORTH LTD.			
	M48	Beautiful Scotland (F)	1939	54.00	36.00
2919	M25	Cavalry	1924	150.00	100.00
	M48	Coastwise (F)	1938	54.00	36.00
1776	25	Comicartoons of Sport	1927	180.00	120.00
	M48	Flying (F)	1938	72.00	48.00
	25	Motor Car Bonnetts	1925	200.00	130.00
3412	25	Old Hostels	1926	190.00	125.00
	M48	Our Countryside (F)	1938	54.00	36.00
	M24	Shots from the Films (F)	1937	75.00	50.00
	?10	Views from the English Lakes	1896	2400.00	1200.00

Ref. No.	No. in Set	Name of Set	Date	COMPLETE SETS Grade 1	COMPLETE SETS Grade 2
		INTERNATIONAL TOBACCO CO. LTD.			
607	28	Domino Cards	1938	9.00	6.00
		Famous Buildings and Monuments Of Britain (Metal Plaques)			
810	30	Series A (Nd. 1-30)	1934	33.00	22.00
3809	L20	Series A (Nd. 31-50)	1934	24.00	16.00
3810	30	Series B (Nd. 51-80)	1934	48.00	32.00
3811	L20	Series B (Nd. 81-100)	1934	33.00	22.00
	100	Film Favourites (Export)	1937	165.00	110.00
1519	A & L100	Gentlemen! The King! (Export) (Black back)	1938	24.00	16.00
A	& L100	Gentlemen! The King! (Blue back) A.A.	1938	42.00	28.00
2083	50	International Code of Signals	1934	24.00	16.00
	48	Screen Lovers	Unissued	150.00	100.00
		JACK & JILL CIGARS (U.S.A.)			
	X25	Actresses (JAKE)	1890	2300.00	1150.00
		PETER JACKSON			
	28	Beautiful Scotland (F)	1939	30.00	20.00
	M48	Beautiful Scotland (F)	1939	51.00	34.00
	28	Coastwise (F)	1938	30.00	20.00
	M48	Coastwise (F)	1938	63.00	42.00
3268	28	Famous Film Stars (F)	1935	90.00	60.00
5476	27	Famous Films (F)	1934	90.00	60.00
2857	28	Film Scenes (F)	1936	90.00	60.00
3914	L28	Film Scenes (Different) (F)	1936	130.00	85.00
	28	Flying (F)	1938	120.00	80.00
	M48	Flying (F)	1938	165.00	110.00
	A & L100	Gentlemen! The King! (Black back Jackson's name)	1937	90.00	60.00
	A & L100	Gentlemen! The King! (Blue back Jackson's name) A.A.	1937	85.00	55.00
	A & L100	Gentlemen! The King! (Overprinted on International black back) A.A.	1937	90.00	60.00
	A & L100	Gentlemen! The King! (Overprinted on International blue back) A.A.	1937	85.00	55.00
	28	Life in the Navy (F)	1937	60.00	40.00
	L28	Life in the Navy (Different) (F)	1937	85.00	55.00

Ref. No.	No. in Set	Name of Set	Date	COMPLETE SETS Grade 1	Grade 2
		PETER JACKSON (Cont'd)			
	28	Our Countryside (F)	1938	30.00	20.00
	M48	Our Countryside (F)	1938	60.00	40.00
2858	28	Shots from the Films (F)	1937	72.00	48.00
2997	M24	Shots from the Films (F)	1937	84.00	56.00
3410	A & L250	Speed Through the Ages (Export)	1937	90.00	60.00
2859	28	Stars in Famous Films (F)	1934	105.00	70.00
1313	A & L150	The Pageant of Kingship (Peter Jackson)	1937	54.00	36.00
	A & L150	The Pageant of Kingship (Peter Jackson, Overseas Ltd., Card) A.A.	1937	75.00	50.00
	A & L150	The Pageant of Kingship (Peter Jackson, Overseas Ltd., Paper) A.A.	1937	75.00	50.00
		LAMBERT & BUTLER			
	20	Actresses (BLARM)	1900	1000.00	500.00
	50	Actors & Actresses "WALP" (Export Issue)	1907	260.00	130.00
	250	Actresses "ALWICS" (Export Issue)	1908	1250.00	625.00
	10	Actresses & Their Autographs (L & B Cigarettes)	1898	2000.00	1000.00
	10	Actresses & Their Autographs (L & B Cigarettes, narrow card) A.A.	1898	2000.00	1000.00
	10	Actresses & Their Autographs (L & B Tobaccos) A.A.	1898	2400.00	1200.00
	10	Actresses & Their Autographs (L & B Tobaccos, narrow card) A.A.	1898	1800.00	900.00
	50	Admirals (Flaked Gold Leaf Honey Dew back)	1900	1420.00	710.00
	50	Admirals (May Blossoms back) A.A.	1900	1420.00	710.00
	50	Admirals (Prize Medal Bird's Eye back) A.A.	1900	1420.00	710.00
942	50	Admirals (Viking back) A.A.	1900	1420.00	710.00
5352	1	Advertisement Card (Spanish Dancer)	1898	650.00	325.00
1102	50	Aeroplane Markings	1937	90.00	50.00
1103	25	A History of Aviation (Green Front)	1932	45.00	30.00
1104	25	A History of Aviation (Brown Front) A.A.	1933	70.00	45.00
1107	40	Arms of the Kings & Queens of England	1906	260.00	130.00
448	25	Aviation	1915	130.00	65.00

Ref. No.	No. in Set	Name of Set	Date	COMPLETE SETS Grade 1	Grade 2

LAMBERT & BUTLER (Cont'd)

Ref. No.	No. in Set	Name of Set	Date	Grade 1	Grade 2
	26	Beauties (HOL) (Flaked Gold Leaf Honey Dew back)	1899	1550.00	775.00
	26	Beauties (HOL) (Log Cabin back) A.A.	1899	1550.00	775.00
	26	Beauties (HOL) (May Blossom back) A.A.	1899	1550.00	775.00
	26	Beauties (HOL) (Viking Navy Cut back) A.A.	1899	1550.00	775.00
	50	Beauties (LAWHA) (Export Issue)	1908	260.00	130.00
1108	50	Birds & Eggs	1906	240.00	120.00
	?25	Boer War & Boxer Rebellion — Sketches	1901	1200.00	600.00
	20	Boer War Generals (CLAM)	1901	1000.00	500.00
	10	Boer War Generals (FLAC)	1901	560.00	280.00
	1	Boer War Series (Col. Baden-Powell)	1901	620.00	310.00
1487	25	British Trees & Their Uses	1937	54.00	36.00
1492	25	Common Fallacies	1928	78.00	48.00
	50	Conundrums (Blue back)	1901	1680.00	840.00
	50	Conundrums (Green back) A.A.	1901	1300.00	650.00
4074	12	Coronation Robes	1902	380.00	190.00
800	25	Dance Band Leaders	1936	120.00	80.00
	83	Danske Byvaabner (Danish)	1911	1600.00	800.00
	28	Dominoes (Packets)	1955	45.00	30.00
1105	50	Empire Air Routes	1936	110.00	65.00
	26	Etchings of Dogs (Export Issue)	1929	600.00	400.00
	L26	Etchings of Dogs (Export Issue) A.A.	1929	825.00	550.00
419	25	Famous British Airmen & Airwomen	1935	40.00	24.00
1412	25	Fauna of Rhodesia	1929	30.00	20.00
2782	50	Find Your Way (back — Box No. 152, Drury Lane)	1932	72.00	48.00
	50	Find Your Way (back — Box No. 152, London) A.A.	1932	72.00	48.00
	50	Find Your Way (back — Overprinted in Red) A.A.	1932	72.00	48.00
934	25	Flag Girls of All Nations (Overseas Issue)	1911	440.00	220.00
608	50	Footballers 1930-31	1931	180.00	120.00
2271	25	Garden Life	1930	34.00	20.00
1491	25	Hints & Tips for Motorists	1929	125.00	75.00
	50	Homeland Events (F)	1925	72.00	48.00
420	50	Horsemanship	1938	110.00	65.00
2998	25	How Motor Cars Work	1931	80.00	50.00
421	50	Interesting Customs of the Navy Army & Air Force	1939	72.00	44.00

A SELECTION FROM LAMBERT & BUTLER

SET No: 420

SET No: 1488

SET No: 19

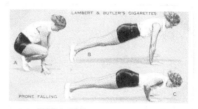

SET No: 559

SET No: 359

SET No: 228

SET No: 1496

SET No: 1490

Ref. No.	No. in Set	Name of Set	Date	COMPLETE SETS Grade 1	Grade 2
		LAMBERT & BUTLER (Cont'd)			
3283	25	Interesting Musical Instruments	1929	90.00	60.00
422	50	Interesting Sidelights on the Work of the G.P.O.	1939	66.00	44.00
	20	International Yachts	1902	1300.00	650.00
1106	25	Japanese Series	1904	350.00	175.00
4173	4	Jockeys (no frame)	1902	260.00	130.00
	10	Jockeys (with frame)	1902	640.00	320.00
559	50	Keep Fit	1937	46.00	26.00
	25	London Characters (no Album Clause)	1934	—	—
1488	25	London Characters (with Album Clause) A.A.	1934	78.00	48.00
	50	London Zoo (Overseas Issue) (F)	1927	66.00	44.00
	50	Merchant Ships of the World (Overseas Issue)	1924	130.00	85.00
5357	25	Motor Car Radiators	1928	165.00	110.00
228	25	Motor Cars 1st Series (Green Back)	1922	120.00	60.00
229	25	Motor Cars 2nd Series (Green Back)	1923	120.00	60.00
1493	50	Motor Cars 3rd Series	1926	280.00	140.00
1494	25	Motor Cars (Grey Back)	1934	115.00	65.00
359	50	Motor Cycles	1923	320.00	160.00
1489	50	Motor Index Marks	1926	140.00	90.00
3108	25	Motors (Text back)	1908	1200.00	600.00
	25	Motors (Plain back) A.A.	1908	—	—
	30	Music Hall Celebrities (Export Issue)	1907	240.00	120.00
1383	25	Naval Portraits (Series of 25)	1914	140.00	70.00
1916	50	Naval Portraits (Series of 50) I.A.	1915	280.00	140.00
19	25	Pirates & Highwaymen	1926	40.00	24.00
	50	Popular Film Stars (Title in 1 Line, Export Issue) (F)	1925	75.00	50.00
	50	Popular Film Stars (Title in 2 Lines, Export Issue) (F) A.A.	1925	68.00	45.00
	50	Popular Film Stars (Variety Cigarettes, Export Issue) (F) A.A.	1925	120.00	80.00
1497	25	Rhodesian Series	1928	40.00	25.00
	100	Royalty, Notabilities & Events 1900-2 (Overseas Issue)	1902	1800.00	900.00
	100	Russo Japanese Series (Overseas Issue)	1903	760.00	380.00
	1	The May Blossom Calendar (Triple Folder)	1900	—	—
	50	The Royal Family at Home & Abroad (Overseas Issue) (F)	1927	54.00	36.00
1496	50	The Thames from Lechlade to London (Text on back)	1907	550.00	275.00

SET No: 1103

SET No: 1107

SET No: 1492

SET No: 1102

SET No: 1105

SET No: 800

SET No: 1487

SET No: 419

Ref. No.	No. in Set	Name of Set	Date	COMPLETE SETS Grade 1	Grade 2
		LAMBERT & BUTLER (Cont'd)			
	50	The Thames from Lechlade to London (Plain back)	1907	—	—
	50	The World of Sport (Overseas Issue) (F)	1927	75.00	50.00
1495	25	Third Rhodesian Series	1930	21.00	14.00
	50	Travellers Tales	Unissued	—	—
	50	Types of Modern Beauty (Overseas Issue) (F)	1927	60.00	40.00
	4	Types of the British Army & Navy (Specialities back)	1897	380.00	190.00
	4	Types of the British Army & Navy (Viking back) A.A.	1897	420.00	210.00
1498	25	Waverley Series	1904	450.00	225.00
	50	Who's Who in Sport (Overseas Issue) (F)	1926	75.00	50.00
1490	25	Winter Sports	1914	130.00	65.00
1534	25	Wireless Telegraphy	1909	200.00	100.00
633	25	Wonders of Nature	1924	25.00	15.00
1111	25	World's Locomotives (Series of 25)	1912	200.00	100.00
1110	50	World's Locomotives (Series of 50) I.A.	1913	400.00	200.00
1112	25	World's Locomotives (1A-25A)	1913	220.00	110.00
		LAMBKIN BROS.			
2589	36	Country Scenes	1924	225.00	150.00
	L36	Country Scenes	1926	255.00	170.00
	?9	Irish Views	1925	240.00	160.00
	?5	Lily of Killarney (Views)	1925	525.00	350.00
		LANCS & YORKS TOBACCO MANUFACTURING CO. LTD., (L. & Y. Tob. Mfg. Co.)			
	26	Actresses (FROGA A)	1901	—	—
		C. & J. LAW			
	25	Types of British Soldiers	1915	1020.00	510.00
	50	War Portraits	1915	5800.00	2900.00

Ref. No.	No. in Set	Name of Set	Date	COMPLETE SETS Grade 1	Grade 2
		R. J. LEA LTD.			
	1	Advertisement Card (Swashbuckler)	1920	—	—
3781	M12	Butterflies & Moths (Silk)	1924	64.00	32.00
3782	L12	Butterflies & Moths (Silk)	1924	64.00	32.00
577	P6	Butterflies & Moths (Silk)	1924	40.00	20.00
	70	Cigarette Transfers (Locomotives)	1916	600.00	300.00
	25	Civilians of Countries Fighting with the Allies	1914	430.00	215.00
2092	48	Coronation Souvenir (Glossy) (F)	1937	26.00	16.00
3632	48	Coronation Souvenir (Matt) (F) A.A.	1937	30.00	20.00
634	M48	Coronation Souvenir (F) A.A.	1937	36.00	24.00
3280	25	Dogs (1-25)	1923	130.00	85.00
2940	25	Dogs (26-50)	1923	175.00	115.00
2393	25	English Birds	1922	85.00	55.00
3650	54	Famous Film Stars (F)	1939	90.00	60.00
3766	48	Famous Racehorses of 1926 (F)	1927	130.00	85.00
634	M48	Famous Racehorses of 1926 (F) A.A.	1927	175.00	115.00
3317	48	Famous Views (F)	1936	15.00	10.00
3772	M48	Famous Views (F) A.A.	1936	30.00	20.00
5491	36	Film Stars 1st Series (F)	1934	115.00	75.00
5492	36	Film Stars 2nd Series (F)	1934	100.00	65.00
2384	25	Fish	1926	51.00	34.00
1538	50	Flowers to Grow (The Best Perennials)	1913	340.00	170.00
5257	48	Girls from the Shows (Glossy) (F)	1935	115.00	75.00
	48	Girls from the Shows (Matt) A.A.	1935	130.00	85.00
1388	50	Miniatures (No Border)	1912	240.00	120.00
1389	50	Miniatures (Gold Border) A.A.	1912	240.00	120.00
1390	50	Miniatures (51-100)	1912	220.00	110.00
3269	46/50	Modern Miniatures (No's 1, 8, 12 & 32 Rare)	1913	110.00	55.00
	12	More Lea's Smokers (Green border)	1905	1450.00	725.00
	12	More Lea's Smokers (Red border) A.A.	1905	1800.00	900.00
1081	50	Old English Pottery & Porcelain	1912	220.00	110.00
1082	50	Old Pottery & Porcelain 2nd Series (Chairman)	1912	150.00	75.00
	50	Old Pottery & Porcelain 2nd Series (Recorder) A.A.	1912	440.00	220.00
1083	50	Old Pottery & Porcelain 3rd Series (Chairman)	1912	150.00	75.00
	50	Old Pottery & Porcelain 3rd Series (Recorder) A.A.	1912	440.00	220.00
1537	50	Old Pottery & Porcelain 4th Series	1913	150.00	75.00
1841	50	Old Pottery & Porcelain 5th Series	1913	150.00	75.00
664	P24	Old English Pottery & Porcelain	1912	280.00	140.00

Ref. No.	No. in Set	Name of Set	Date	**COMPLETE SETS** Grade 1	Grade 2
		R. J. LEA LTD. (Cont'd)			
3601	54	Old Pottery (Silk)	1914	120.00	60.00
3602	72	Old Pottery (Silk, different)	1914	140.00	70.00
3270	54	Radio Stars (Glossy front) (F)	1935	135.00	90.00
	54	Radio Stars (Matt front) A.A.	1935	145.00	95.00
3342	50	Regimental Crests & Badges 1st Series (Silk) (without Chairman backs)	1923	100.00	50.00
	50	Regimental Crests & Badges 2nd Series (Silk) (Chairman backs)	1923	140.00	70.00
3318	50	Roses	1924	72.00	48.00
1928	50	Ships of the World	1925	120.00	80.00
3765	25	The Evolution of the Royal Navy	1925	60.00	40.00
568	25	War Pictures	1915	180.00	90.00
1653	25	War Portraits	1915	210.00	105.00
665	48	Wonders of the World (Glossy) (F)	1938	24.00	16.00
	48	Wonders of the World (Matt) A.A.	1938	36.00	24.00
2357	M48	Wonders of the World (F) A.A.	1938	30.00	20.00
		ALFRED L. LEAVER			
	B12	Manikin Cards	1922	1120.00	560.00
		J. LEES			
	?21	Northampton Town Football Club (Nd. 301-321)	1915	2500.00	1250.00
		LEON DE CUBA CIGARS			
	30	Colonial Troops	1902	5200.00	2600.00
		A. LEWIS & CO. (WESTMINSTER) LTD.			
3357	52	Horoscopes	1938	75.00	50.00
	50	War Portraits (Sepia)	1915	—	—

I. LEWIS & CO. (U.S.A.)
LIGGETT & MYERS TOBACCO CO. (U.S.A.)

A SELECTION FROM LEA & RICHARD LLOYD

SET No: 1083

SET No: 1537

SET No: 1841

SET No: 1963

SET No: 568

SET No: 658

SET No: 512

SET No: 1653

Ref. No.	No. in Set	Name of Set	Date	**COMPLETE SETS**	
				Grade 1	Grade 2
		LEWIS & ALLEN CO. (U.S.A.)			
	X250	Views & Art Studies	1912	2200.00	1100.00
		H. C. LLOYD & SONS LTD.			
	28	Academy Gems (Green front)	1901	2300.00	1150.00
	28	Academy Gems (Purple front) A.A.	1901	2300.00	1150.00
	28	Academy Gems (Reddish-Brown front) A.A.	1901	2300.00	1150.00
	26	Actresses & Boer War Celebrities	1901	1950.00	975.00
709	B?35	Devon Footballers & Boer War Celebrities	1902	—	—
	25	Star Girls	1899	—	—
	L36	War Pictures	1915	6800.00	3400.00
		RICHARD LLOYD & SONS			
	?20	Actresses, Celebrities & Yachts	1900	3000.00	1500.00
1963	25	Atlantic Records	1936	75.00	50.00
	25	Boer War Celebrities	1899	1550.00	775.00
5643	27	Cinema Stars (1-27) (F)	1935	210.00	140.00
658	27	Cinema Stars (28-54) (F)	1935	36.00	18.00
3764	27	Cinema Stars, 3rd Series (55-81) (F)	1936	210.00	140.00
512	25	Cinema Stars (Matt front)	1938	48.00	24.00
652	25	Famous Cricketers Puzzle Series	1930	150.00	100.00
	96	National Types, Costumes & Flags	1900	5000.00	2500.00
278	25	Old English Inns	1923	50.00	30.00
1921	25	Old Inns, (Series 2)	1924	95.00	60.00
2676	50	Old Inns, A.A. 2 Sets	1925	60.00	40.00
2576	10	Scenes from San Toy	1905	170.00	85.00
791	25	Tricks and Puzzles	1935	18.00	12.00
655	25	Types of Horses	1926	81.00	54.00
3482	25	Zoo Series	1926	28.00	18.00
		MARCOVITCH & CO.			
802	18	Beauties (Plain Back) (F)	1932	18.00	12.00
477	L7	The Story in Red & White	1955	18.00	12.00

Ref. No.	No. in Set	Name of Set	Date	Grade 1	Grade 2
		J. MILLHOFF & CO. LTD.			
1275	54	Antique Pottery (F)	1927	60.00	40.00
2242	M56	Antique Pottery (F)	1927	63.00	42.00
2442	30	Art Treasures	1927	33.00	22.00
1199	L50	Art Treasures 1st Series	1926	36.00	24.00
1312	L25	Art Treasures 2nd Series	1928	27.00	18.00
1197	L25	England Historic & Picturesque 1st Series	1928	29.00	19.00
1198	L25	England Historic & Picturesque 2nd Series	1928	29.00	19.00
1673	27	Famous Golfers (F)	1928	270.00	180.00
	27	Famous Test Cricketers (F)	1928	145.00	95.00
3725	M27	Famous Test Cricketers (F) A.A.	1928	145.00	95.00
	L40	Film Series 1 (Dutch)	1923	375.00	250.00
	L60	Film Series 1 (Dutch)	1923	565.00	375.00
	L60	Film Series 2 (Dutch)	1924	565.00	375.00
	L25	Film Series 3 (Dutch)	1924	270.00	180.00
	?M244	Film Series 4 (Dutch) (F)	1925	1800.00	1200.00
	M105	Film Series 4 (Dutch) (F)	1925	765.00	525.00
5243	M25	Gallery Pictures	1929	39.00	26.00
672	50	Geographia Map Series (Sectional)	1931	90.00	60.00
1406	36	In the Public Eye (F)	1930	54.00	36.00
3895	25	Men of Genius	1924	170.00	85.00
276	L25	Picturesque Old England	1931	33.00	22.00
528	27	Real Photographs Series (Glossy) (F)	1931	9.00	6.00
	27	Real Photographs A Series (Matt) (F) A.A.	1931	19.00	12.50
1087	27	Real Photographs 2nd Series (F)	1931	15.00	10.00
1088	27	Real Photographs 3rd Series (F)	1932	11.50	7.50
1089	27	Real Photographs 4th Series (F)	1933	11.50	7.50
1090	27	Real Photographs 5th Series (F)	1933	15.00	10.00
1091	27	Real Photographs 6th Series (F)	1933	15.00	10.00
487	25	Reproductions of Celebrated Oil Paintings	1928	60.00	30.00
	74	"RILEITE" Miniature Pictures	1925	—	—
1507	L25	Roses	1927	60.00	40.00
	?70	Sports Series (Dutch) (F)	1925	1425.00	950.00
	?L8	Theatre Advertisement Cards	1905	1200.00	600.00
	?P4	Theatre Advertisement Cards	1905	800.00	400.00
1248	54	The Homeland Series (F)	1933	18.00	12.00
2864	M56	The Homeland Series (F) I.A.	1933	18.00	12.00
1624	50	Things to Make	1935	36.00	24.00
2427	50	What the Stars Say	1934	30.00	20.00
1530	36	Zoological Studies (F)	1929	10.50	7.00

Ref. No.	No. in Set	Name of Set	Date	COMPLETE SETS	
				Grade 1	Grade 2
		STEPHEN MITCHELL & SON			
	?51	Actors & Actresses (FROGA Coloured)	1899	1500.00	750.00
	26	Actors & Actresses (FROGA B) (Brown)	1899	820.00	410.00
	26	Actors & Actresses (FROGA C) (Coloured)	1899	820.00	410.00
	50	Actors & Actresses (FROGA D)	1899	1480.00	740.00
	1	Advertisement Card (Maid of Honour)	1900	640.00	320.00
3613	50	A Gallery of 1934	1935	144.00	96.00
1500	50	A Gallery of 1935	1936	150.00	75.00
783	50	Air Raid Precautions	1938	60.00	40.00
1501	30	A Model Army	1932	45.00	30.00
413	25	Angling	1928	140.00	90.00
1392	50	Arms & Armour	1916	340.00	170.00
1393	25	Army Ribbons & Buttons	1916	160.00	80.00
680	50	A Road Map of Scotland (Small numerals)	1933	96.00	64.00
	50	A Road Map of Scotland (Large numerals in circles) A.A.	1933	96.00	64.00
	50	A Road Map of Scotland (Overprinted in Red) A.A.	1933	112.00	74.00
	25	Boxer Rebellion (Sketches)	1901	960.00	480.00
1499	25	British Warships 1st Series	1915	300.00	150.00
1078	25	British Warships 2nd Series	1915	300.00	150.00
2753	50	Clan Tartans 1st Series	1927	105.00	70.00
225	25	Clan Tartans 2nd Series	1927	36.00	18.00
471	25	Empire Exhibition, Scotland	1938	18.00	12.00
360	25	Famous Crosses	1923	18.00	12.00
414	50	Famous Scots	1933	50.00	30.00
1502	50	First Aid	1938	54.00	36.00
	P3	Glasgow International Exhibition 1901	1901	300.00	150.00
2290	50	Humorous Drawings	1924	135.00	90.00
	50	Interesting Buildings	1905	500.00	250.00
484	40	London Ceremonials	1928	75.00	45.00
1080	25	Medals	1916	190.00	95.00
1765	25	Money	1913	190.00	95.00
415	25	Old Sporting Prints	1930	48.00	24.00
460	50	Our Empire	1937	30.00	20.00
1929	25	Regimental Crests & Collar Badges	1900	470.00	235.00
1503	70	River & Coastal Steamers	1925	280.00	140.00
1414	50	Scotland's Story	1929	180.00	90.00
2289	25	Scottish Clan Series	1903	460.00	230.00

A SELECTION FROM MILLHOFF & MITCHELL

SET No: 1406

SET No: 2442

SET No: 484

SET No: 3613

SET No: 414

SET No: 471

SET No: 1500

SET No: 1501

Ref. No.	No. in Set	Name of Set	Date	COMPLETE SETS Grade 1	Grade 2

STEPHEN MITCHELL & SON (Cont'd)

Ref. No.	No. in Set	Name of Set	Date	Grade 1	Grade 2
3909	50	Scottish Footballers	1934	130.00	80.00
2359	50	Scottish Football Snaps	1935	125.00	75.00
870	25	Seals	1911	190.00	95.00
2488	25	Sports	1907	550.00	275.00
464	25	Stars of Screen History	1939	60.00	36.00
1079	25	Statues & Monuments	1914	180.00	90.00
3783	50	The World of Tomorrow	1936	66.00	42.00
803	25	Village Models Series 1	1925	60.00	40.00
681	L25	Village Models Series 1 A.A.	1925	115.00	75.00
1504	25	Village Model Series 2	1925	70.00	45.00
682	L25	Village Model Series 2 A.A.	1925	120.00	80.00
275	50	Wonderful Century	1937	50.00	30.00

MOORGATE TOBACCO CO. LTD.

Ref. No.	No. in Set	Name of Set	Date	Grade 1	Grade 2
2501 L & A30		The New Elizabethan Age (Matt front)	1953	110.00	70.00
L & A30		The New Elizabethan Age (varnished front) A.A.	1953	85.00	55.00

B. MORRIS & SONS LTD.

Ref. No.	No. in Set	Name of Set	Date	Grade 1	Grade 2
3662	30	Actresses (Black & White)	1898	110.00	55.00
	26	Actresses & Beauties (FROGA A)	1899	1300.00	650.00
	L26	Actresses (FROGA B)	1899	—	—
	1	Advertisement Card (Soldier & Girl)	1900	520.00	260.00
1099	50	Animals at the Zoo (Blue Back)	1924	45.00	30.00
1098	50	Animals at the Zoo (Grey Back) A.A.	1924	55.00	35.00
2294	35	At the London Zoo Aquarium	1928	24.00	14.00
4148	25	Australian Cricketers	1925	110.00	65.00
	M24	Battleship Crests (Silk)	1916	1060.00	530.00
	?50	Beauties (CHOAB)	1898	3400.00	1700.00
	?45	Beauties Collotype	1898	—	—
	21	Beauties "MOM"	1899	1050.00	525.00
	20	Boer War (V.C. Heroes)	1900	1350.00	675.00
	25	Boer War Celebrities (PAM)	1901	1120.00	560.00
2065	25	Captain Blood	1937	40.00	24.00
3604	M25	English & Foreign Birds (Silk)	1924	170.00	85.00
516	L25	English Flowers (Silk)	1915	140.00	70.00
3603	L50	English Flowers (Silk) I.A.	1915	320.00	160.00
2892	50	Film Star Series	1923	200.00	120.00
2441	30	General Interest	1910	320.00	160.00
1100	25	Golf Stroke Series	1923	130.00	80.00
2088	12	Horoscopes	1936	12.00	6.00
459	25	How Films are Made	1934	40.00	24.00

A SELECTION FROM MITCHELL

SET No: 225

SET No: 2359

SET No: 464

SET No: 415

SET No: 2290

SET No: 460

SET No: 1503

SET No: 275

Ref. No.	No. in Set	Name of Set	Date	Grade 1 (COMPLETE SETS)	Grade 2 (COMPLETE SETS)
		B. MORRIS & SONS LTD.(Cont'd)			
2360	50	How to Sketch	1929	60.00	40.00
	20	London Views	1904	900.00	450.00
1843	25	Marvels of the Universe	1912	160.00	80.00
2140	25	Measurement of Time	1924	46.00	26.00
770	25	Motor Series	1922	120.00	72.00
1934	50	National & Colonial Arms	1917	480.00	240.00
839	25	Racing Greyhounds (Forcasta Back)	1939	44.00	24.00
	L25	Regimental Colours (Silk)	1917	110.00	55.00
2867	25	Shadowgraphs	1925	63.00	42.00
2295	25	The Queen's Dolls House	1925	90.00	60.00
2066	13	Treasure Island	1924	12.00	8.00
1629	50	Victory Signs Series	1928	36.00	20.00
	25	War Celebrities	1916	230.00	115.00
2296	25	War Pictures	1915	300.00	150.00
454	25	Wax Art Series	1931	15.00	10.00
1101	25	Whipsnade Zoo	1932	12.00	8.00
1518	25	Wireless Series	1923	105.00	70.00
		MOUSTAFA LTD.			
	50	Camera Studies (F)	1923	175.00	115.00
	25	Cinema Stars	1924	160.00	105.00
2282	40	Leo Chambers Dogs Heads	1924	170.00	90.00
	25	Pictures of World Interest	1923	100.00	65.00
2093	25	Real Photos (F)	1925	12.00	8.00
		MURRAY SONS & CO.			
	20	Actresses (BLARM) (Pineapple Cigs. back)	1902	2600.00	1300.00
	20	Actresses (BLARM) (Special Crown Cigs. back) A.A.	1902	3000.00	1500.00
	22	Bathing Beauties (F)	1929	150.00	100.00
1267	40	Bathing Belles	1939	12.00	7.00
	?15	Chess & Draughts Problems	1912	1240.00	620.00
	22	Cinema Scenes (F)	1929	150.00	100.00
	20	Cricketers — black & white (Series H)	1914	2400.00	1200.00
	20	Cricketers — brown (Series H) A.A.	1914	3600.00	1800.00
	25	Crossword Puzzles	1923	2500.00	1250.00
	26	Dancers (F)	1929	175.00	115.00
3291	25	Dancing Girls (back — Belfast Ireland) (F) A.A.	1929	90.00	60.00

Ref. No.	No. in Set	Name of Set	Date	COMPLETE SETS Grade 1	Grade 2

MURRAY SONS & CO. (Cont'd)

Ref. No.	No. in Set	Name of Set	Date	Grade 1	Grade 2
	25	Dancing Girls (back — London & Belfast) (F) A.A.	1929	80.00	50.00
	26	Dancing Girls (back inscribed "Series of 26") (F) I.A.	1929	100.00	65.00
	B16	Flags (Silk)	1911	400.00	200.00
	X3	Flags & Arms (Silks)	1911	320.00	160.00
	34	Footballers (Series H)	1914	1100.00	550.00
	104	Footballers (Series J)	1913	—	—
	?17	Football Flags (Shaped) (Maple Cigs. front)	1906	1250.00	625.00
	?17	Football Flags (Shaped) (Murray's Cigs. front) A.A.	1906	1250.00	625.00
	25	Football Rules	1911	1050.00	525.00
	20	Holidays by the L.M.S.	1927	280.00	180.00
	20	Inventors Series	1924	100.00	65.00
	25	Irish Scenery — Nd. 101-125 (back — Hall Mark Cigs.)	1905	920.00	460.00
	25	Irish Scenery — Nd. 101-125 (back — Pine Apple Cigs.) A.A.	1905	920.00	460.00
	25	Irish Scenery — Nd. 101-125 (back — Special Crown Cigs.) A.A.	1905	920.00	460.00
	25	Irish Scenery — Nd. 101-125 (back — Straight Cut Cigs.) A.A.	1905	920.00	460.00
	25	Irish Scenery — Nd. 101-125 (back — Yachtman Cigs.) A.A.	1905	920.00	460.00
	?31	Orders of Chivalry (Silk)	1925	960.00	480.00
	25	Polo Pictures (E Series)	1910	950.00	475.00
5259	50	Prominent Politicians — B Series (two strengths back)	1909	200.00	100.00
	50	Prominent Politicians — B Series (without above) A.A.	1909	—	—
	50	Puzzle Series (with coupon)	1929	750.00	500.00
	50	Puzzle Series (without coupon) A.A.	1929	210.00	140.00
	B25	Regimental Badges (Silk)	1910	750.00	375.00
	25	Reproductions of Famous Works of Art	1910	—	—
	25	Reproductions of High Class Works of Art	1910	500.00	250.00
4017	50	Stage & Film Stars	1926	165.00	110.00
2089	25	Steamships	1939	30.00	20.00
434	50	The Story of Ships	1940	16.00	8.00
1266	25	Types of Aeroplanes	1929	33.00	22.00
	20	Types of Dogs	1924	120.00	80.00
	35	War Series K	1915	1250.00	625.00
2293	25	War Series L (Nd. 100-124)	1916	130.00	65.00

Ref. No.	No. in Set	Name of Set	Date	COMPLETE SETS Grade 1	Grade 2
		W. H. NEWMAN			
	18	Motor Cycle Series	1913	2400.00	1200.00
		THOS. NICHOLLS & CO.			
	50	Orders of Chivalry	1916	380.00	190.00
		THE NILMA TOBACCO CO.			
	40	Home & Colonial Regiments (Back Marked Series of 70)	1901	5000.00	2500.00
	30	Proverbs	1901	3700.00	1850.00
		M. E. NOTARAS LTD.			
2067	B24	Chinese Scenes	1938	10.50	7.00
2193	36	National Types of Beauty (F)	1939	36.00	18.00
		OGDEN'S LTD. (Including Overseas Issues) Polo Cigarettes issued in Burma, Ceylon, Indian & Malaya Guinea Gold Cigarettes issued in New Zealand Ruler Cigarettes issued in India Tab Cigarettes issued in India & Malaya			
2249	25	ABC of Sport	1927	85.00	55.00
466	50	Actors — Natural & Character Studies	1938	66.00	42.00
	51	Actresses, Black & White (Polo Cigs.)	1907	260.00	130.00
	30	Actresses, Brown (Polo Cigs.)	1908	130.00	65.00
	?200	Actesses, Collotype	1895	14000.00	7000.00
	?25	Actresses (Coloured No Glycerine Back)	1896	4200.00	2100.00
	50	Actresses (Green Gravure)	1898	800.00	400.00
	?200	Actresses & Beauties (Woodbury type)	1895	12000.00	6000.00
2250	50	AFC Nicknames	1933	260.00	130.00
3383	50	Air Raid Precautions	1938	48.00	24.00
	17	Animals (Polo Cigs.)	1916	350.00	175.00
	60	Animals — Cut-Outs (Ruler Cigs.)	1912	280.00	140.00
	60	Animals — Cut-Outs (Tab Cigs.) A.A.	1913	280.00	140.00
1581	50	Applied Electricity	1928	78.00	48.00

SET No: 1578

SET No: 6

SET No: 1616

SET No: 1066

SET No: 509

SET No: 1403

SET No: 1064

SET No: 1478

SET No: 1784

Ref. No.	No. in Set	Name of Set	Date	COMPLETE SETS Grade 1	Grade 2
		OGDEN'S LTD. (Cont'd) (Including Overseas Issues)			
	192	Army Crests & Mottoes	1902	1400.00	700.00
1919	36	Australian Test Cricketers	1928	165.00	110.00
	50	Aviation Series (Tab Cigs.)	1912	420.00	210.00
	28	Beauties (BOCCA)	1899	1140.00	570.00
	50	Beauties (CHOAB)	1899	2300.00	1150.00
	26	Beauties — HOL (Blue Castle back)	1899	820.00	410.00
	26	Beauties — HOL (rubber-stamped Guinea Gold) A.A.	1899	—	—
	100	Beauties, Green Net back (coloured front)	1901	3800.00	1900.00
	66	Beauties, Green Net back (Grey-Sepia front) A.A.	1901	1250.00	625.00
	45	Beauties — Picture Hats (Polo Cigs.)	1911	500.00	250.00
	52	Beauties (P/C Inset)	1899	2500.00	1250.00
	26	Beauties (without P/C Inset) A.A.	1899	1650.00	825.00
3928	50	Beauty Series (numbered) (F)	1900	200.00	100.00
	50	Beauty Series (un-numbered) (F) A.A.	1900	—	—
	52	Beauties & Military (P/C Inset)	1898	2800.00	1400.00
	50	Best Dogs of Their Breed (Blue back Polo Cigs.)	1916	750.00	375.00
	50	Best Dogs of Their Breed (Pink back Polo Cigs.) A.A.	1916	750.00	375.00
1057	50	Billiards by Tom Newman	1928	120.00	60.00
1055	50	Bird's Eggs	1904	150.00	75.00
1050	50	Bird's Eggs (Cut-Outs)	1923	64.00	32.00
	52	Birds of Brilliant Plumage (Ruler Cigs.)	1914	270.00	135.00
	?145	Boer War & General Interest (F)	1901	700.00	350.00
	?50	Boer War & General Interest (F)	1901	2400.00	1200.00
1746	50	Boxers	1915	450.00	225.00
1680	25	Boxing	1914	200.00	100.00
	?P4	Boxing Girls	1900	—	—
1053	50	Boy Scouts (Blue back)	1911	230.00	115.00
	50	Boy Scouts (Green back) A.A.	1911	320.00	160.00
1790	50	Boy Scouts 2nd Series (Blue back)	1912	230.00	115.00
507	50	Boy Scouts 2nd Series (Green back) A.A.	1912	320.00	160.00
1791	50	Boy Scouts 3rd Series (Blue back)	1912	230.00	115.00
	50	Boy Scouts 3rd Series (Green back) A.A.	1912	320.00	160.00
1681	50	Boy Scouts 4th Series (Green back)	1913	220.00	110.00
1793	25	Boy Scouts 5th Series (Green back)	1914	140.00	70.00
1542	50	Boy Scouts (Different)	1929	100.00	60.00

A SELECTION FROM OGDEN'S

SET No: 1050

SET No: 1790

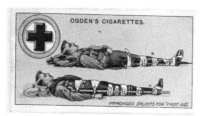

SET No: 1791

SET No: 446

SET No: 1796

SET No: 654

SET No: 1542

SET No: 2058

Ref. No.	No. in Set	Name of Set	Date	Grade 1	Grade 2
		COMPLETE SETS			
		OGDEN'S LTD. (Cont'd)			
		(Including Overseas Issues)			
1051	50	British Birds 1st Series	1905	150.00	75.00
1052	50	British Birds 2nd Series	1908	180.00	90.00
386	50	British Birds (Cut-Outs)	1923	48.00	24.00
654	50	British Birds & Their Eggs	1939	160.00	80.00
1579	50	British Costumes from 100 BC to 1904	1905	600.00	300.00
	25	British Trees & Their Uses			
		(Guinea Gold Cigs.)	1928	60.00	40.00
2058	50	Broadcasting	1935	63.00	42.00
397	50	By the Roadside	1932	78.00	48.00
1447	44	Captains of Association			
		Football Clubs & Colours	1926	180.00	90.00
1796	50	Cathedrals & Abbeys	1936	60.00	40.00
504	50	Champions of 1936	1937	90.00	60.00
1060	50	Children of All Nations (Cut-Outs)	1924	36.00	24.00
	25	China's Ancient Warriors (Ruler Cigs.)	1913	200.00	100.00
2916	50	Club Badges	1914	380.00	190.00
446	50	Colour in Nature	1932	72.00	48.00
	25	Comic Pictures	1898	—	—
3250	50	Construction of Railway Trains	1930	180.00	90.00
2251	50	Coronation Procession (Sect)	1937	80.00	50.00
	12	Cricketers & Footballers (Women)	1897	7200.00	3600.00
	50	Cricketers & Sportsmen	1898	6200.00	3100.00
22	50	Cricket 1926	1926	170.00	110.00
675	25	Derby Entrants 1926	1926	110.00	70.00
676	50	Derby Entrants 1928	1928	125.00	75.00
677	50	Derby Entrants 1929	1929	145.00	90.00
2059	50	Dogs	1936	130.00	80.00
	55	Dominoes (Black back)	1909	130.00	65.00
	28	Dominoes (Actresses FROGA)	1900	—	—
	28	Dominoes (Beauties MOM)	1900	—	—
1410	25	Famous Dirt Track Riders	1929	150.00	75.00
1476	50	Famous Footballers	1908	270.00	135.00
32	25	Famous Railway Trains			
		(Guinea Gold Cigs.)	1927	110.00	60.00
21	50	Famous Rugby Players	1926	125.00	75.00
1617	50	Flags & Funnels of Leading			
		Steamship Lines	1906	380.00	190.00
	20	Flowers (Polo Cigs.)	1915	180.00	90.00
2719	50	Football Caricatures	1935	140.00	80.00
	43	Football Club Badges			
		(Shaped for Buttonholes)	1910	380.00	190.00
1481	50	Football Club Captains	1935	120.00	70.00

A SELECTION OF MARITIME SETS

SET 178

MURRAY SET 434

PLAYER SET 943

GODFREY PHILLIPS SET 253

SET 324

SET 398

SET 1503

SET 20

COMPLETE SETS

Ref. No.	No. in Set	Name of Set	Date	Grade 1	Grade 2
		OGDEN'S LTD. (Cont'd)			
		(Including Overseas Issues)			
1578	51	Football Club Colours	1906	260.00	130.00
6	50	Foreign Birds	1924	50.00	30.00
1066	50	Fowls, Pigeons & Dogs	1904	270.00	135.00
1616	25	Greyhound Racing 1st Series	1927	125.00	75.00
1411	25	Greyhound Racing 2nd Series	1928	125.00	75.00
	1	History of the Union Jack			
		(Folding Card)	1901	220.00	110.00
2060	50	How to Swim	1935	36.00	24.00
	25	Indian Women (Polo Cigs.)	1919	230.00	115.00
1582	50	Infantry Training	1915	170.00	85.00
1059	50	Jockeys & Owners Colours	1927	200.00	100.00
509	50	Jockeys 1930	1930	200.00	100.00
1403	50	Leaders of Men	1924	160.00	80.00
1064	25	Marvels of Motion	1928	75.00	50.00
	52	Miniature Playing Cards			
		(Actresses & Beauties)	1900	340.00	170.00
2432	K52	Miniature Playing Cards (Coolie)	1904	220.00	110.00
	K52	Miniature Playing Cards (Tab)	1909	250.00	125.00
	52	Miniature Playing Cards			
		(Polo Cigs.)	1922	1000.00	500.00
1478	50	Modern British Pottery	1925	70.00	40.00
1477	50	Modern Railways	1936	155.00	85.00
1580	50	Modern War Weapons	1915	220.00	110.00
1784	25	Modes of Conveyance	1927	95.00	55.00
2253	50	Motor Races 1931	1931	170.00	100.00
	30	Music Hall Celebrities (Polo Cigs.)	1911	280.00	140.00
	50	Music Hall Celebrities (Tab Cigs)	1911	420.00	210.00
398	50	Ocean Greyhounds	1938	96.00	48.00
2252	25	Optical Illusions	1923	70.00	45.00
1391	50	Orders of Chivalry	1907	240.00	120.00
1937	25	Owners Racing Colours & Jockeys			
		(Green back)	1914	160.00	80.00
1067	50	Owners Racing Colours & Jockeys			
		(Blue back)	1906	250.00	125.00
399	25	Picturesque People of the Empire	1927	50.00	30.00
2254	50	Picturesque Villages	1936	60.00	40.00
1936	25	Poultry (Ogdens on Front)	1915	120.00	60.00
33	25	Poultry (No Ogdens on Front) A.A.	1915	130.00	65.00
1927	25	Poultry 2nd Series	1916	120.00	60.00
3678	25	Poultry Alphabet	1924	84.00	48.00
1061	25	Poultry Rearing & Management			
		1st Series	1922	90.00	45.00

A SELECTION FROM PATTREIOUEX ETC.

SET No: 400

SET No: 710

SET No: 711

SET No: 2483

SET No: 1054

SET No: 519

SET No: 248

SET No: 661

Ref. No.	No. in Set	Name of Set	Date	COMPLETE SETS Grade 1	Grade 2
		OGDEN'S LTD. (Cont'd) (Including Overseas Issues)			
1062	25	Poultry Rearing & Management 2nd Series	1923	90.00	45.00
1068	50	Prominent Cricketers of 1938	1938	130.00	70.00
490	50	Prominent Racehorses of 1933	1934	150.00	75.00
1535	50	Pugilists & Wrestlers 1st Series	1908	250.00	125.00
884	25	Pugilists & Wrestlers 2nd Series	1909	160.00	80.00
1404	50	Pugilists in Action	1928	220.00	110.00
570	50	Racehorses	1907	260.00	130.00
1063	50	Racing Pigeons	1931	180.00	110.00
2256	25	Records of the World	1908	110.00	55.00
	50	Riders of the World (Polo Cigs.)	1911	340.00	170.00
1065	50	Royal Mail	1909	380.00	190.00
	50	Russo Japanese Series	1904	1900.00	950.00
1056	50	Sea Adventure	1939	22.00	12.00
3002	50	Sectional Cycling Map	1910	200.00	100.00
1689	50	Shakespeare Series (numbered)	1905	1020.00	510.00
	50	Shakespeare Series (un-numbered) A.A.	1905	960.00	480.00
	36	Ships & Their Pennants (Polo Cigs.)	1911	350.00	175.00
502	50	Shots from the Films	1936	110.00	65.00
535	25	Sights of London	1923	40.00	26.00
2255	50	Smugglers & Smuggling	1932	110.00	65.00
1381	50	Soldiers of the King	1909	440.00	220.00
1480	50	Steeplechase Celebrities	1931	155.00	85.00
1751	50	Steeplechase Trainers & Owners Colours	1927	140.00	80.00
1058	50	Swimming, Diving & Life Saving	1931	70.00	40.00
4190	25	Swiss Views 1-25	1910	130.00	65.00
890	25	Swiss Views 26-50	1910	240.00	120.00
1750	50	The Blue Riband of the Atlantic	1929	200.00	100.00
400	50	The Story of Sand	1934	70.00	40.00
15	25	Trainers & Owners Colours 1st Series	1925	80.00	50.00
36	25	Trainers & Owners Colours 2nd Series	1926	85.00	55.00
	32	Transport of the World (Polo Cigs)	1917	320.00	160.00
519	50	Trick Billiards	1934	95.00	55.00
1054	50	Turf Personalities	1929	205.00	105.00
3222	48	V.C. Heroes	1901	1000.00	500.00
1749	25	Whaling	1927	100.00	60.00
1618	50	Yachts & Motor Boats	1930	135.00	85.00
444	50	Zoo Studies	1937	45.00	30.00

Ref. No.	No. in Set	Name of Set	Date	COMPLETE SETS Grade 1	Grade 2

Ogdens Guinea Gold and Tab Issues are not stock items but regularly appear in our Postal Auctions — see page 22.

J. A. PATTREIOUEX LTD.

Ref. No.	No. in Set	Name of Set	Date	Grade 1	Grade 2
	96	Animals (CA1-CA96) (F)	1922	98.00	65.00
	L50	Animals & Scenes (1-50) (F)	1925	66.00	44.00
	96	Animals & Scenes (CC1-CC96) (F)	1926	90.00	60.00
	96	Animals & Scenes (JS1-96A) (F)	1928	90.00	60.00
	96	Animals & Scenes (250-345) (F)	1924	90.00	60.00
	96	Amimals & Scenes (346-441) (F)	1925	90.00	60.00
	L50	Animals & Scenes (F)	1925	60.00	40.00
	50	Animal Studies (A42-A91)	1923	45.00	30.00
	50	Animal Studies (A92-A141)	1924	45.00	30.00
	50	Animal Studies (A151-A200)	1925	45.00	30.00
	L30	Beauties (JM1-JM30) (F)	1929	90.00	60.00
2081	28	Beautiful Scotland (F)	1939	32.00	20.00
70	M48	Beautiful Scotland (F)	1939	16.00	10.00
71	M48	Britain from the Air (F)	1939	14.00	9.00
	L50	British & Egyptian Scenes (CM1-50A) (F)	1927	60.00	40.00
	L50	British Empire Exhibition (JM1-50B) (F)	1928	84.00	56.00
5218	50	British Empire Exhibition Series	1929	105.00	70.00
72	M48	British Railways (F)	1938	40.00	25.00
2418	50	Builders of the British Empire	1929	165.00	110.00
	X24	Cadet's Jackpot Jigsaws	1969	21.00	14.00
	X100	Cathedrals, Etc. (SJ1-SJ100) (F)	1927	180.00	120.00
3321	50	Celebrities in Sport	1930	175.00	115.00
	L30	Child Studies (JM No. 1-JM30) (F)	1928	120.00	80.00
2082	28	Coastwise (F)	1939	30.00	20.00
77	M48	Coastwise (F)	1939	14.00	9.00
2503	75	Cricketers Series	1928	900.00	525.00
	96	Cricketers (C1-C96) Printed back (F)	1926	7000.00	3500.00
	96	Cricketers (C1-C96) Plain back (F) A.A.	1926	7000.00	3500.00
	50	Dirt Track Riders	1929	550.00	350.00
	54	Dirt Track Riders (Descriptive back) (F)	1930	750.00	475.00
	54	Dirt Track Riders (Non Descriptive back) (F) A.A.	1930	1700.00	1100.00
248	M48	Dogs (F)	1939	25.00	15.00
789	30	Drawing Made Easy	1930	93.00	62.00

Ref. No.	No. in Set	Name of Set	Date	COMPLETE SETS Grade 1	Grade 2
		J. A. PATTREIOUEX LTD. (Cont'd)			
	L50	Famous Statues (JCM1-50C) (F)	1927	90.00	60.00
	28	Flying (F)	1938	60.00	40.00
661	M48	Flying (F)	1938	30.00	20.00
	96	Footballers (F1-F96) (F)	1927	450.00	300.00
	96	Footballers (F97-F192) (F)	1927	450.00	300.00
	96	Footballers (FA1-96) (F)	1927	400.00	250.00
	96	Footballers (FB1-96) (F)	1928	400.00	250.00
	96	Footballers (FC1-96) (F)	1928	400.00	250.00
2521	78	Footballers in Action (F)	1934	270.00	170.00
	100	Footballers Series (Captions in Brown)	1927	675.00	450.00
	50	Footballers Series (Captions in Blue)	1927	400.00	260.00
	L50	Football Teams (F193-F242) (F)	1927	675.00	450.00
662	M48	Holiday Haunts by the Sea (F)	1937	14.00	9.00
	25	King Lud Problems	1936	360.00	240.00
710	26	Maritime Flags	1931	270.00	180.00
	96	Natives & Scenes (1-96B) (F)	1926	99.00	66.00
	36	Natives & Scenes (1-36B) (F) A.A.	1926	39.00	26.00
	96	Natives & Scenes (CB1-CB96) (F) A.A.	1926	99.00	66.00
	96	Natives & Scenes (JS1-96) (F) A.A.	1926	99.00	66.00
	28	Our Countryside (F)	1938	30.00	20.00
78	M48	Our Countryside (F)	1938	14.00	9.00
	L50	Overseas Scenes (CM1-50B)	1926	60.00	40.00
	L50	Overseas Scenes (JM1-50) A.A.	1927	60.00	40.00
	L50	Overseas Scenes (CM1-50B) (F)	1927	60.00	40.00
	L50	Overseas Scenes (S101-S150) A.A.	1928	60.00	40.00
	96	Overseas Scenes (1-96D) (F)	1927	90.00	60.00
	L50	Overseas Scenes (1-50E) (F)	1929	65.00	45.00
	L50	Overseas Scenes (1-50F) (F)	1929	65.00	45.00
	L50	Overseas Scenes (JM1-50) (F)	1929	65.00	45.00
	25	Photos of Football Stars	1929	750.00	500.00
2483	50	Railway Posters by Famous Artists	1930	425.00	275.00
	54	Real Photographs of London (F)	1936	120.00	80.00
	L50	Scenes (201-250) (F)	1925	60.00	40.00
	L50	Scenes (G1-50) (F)	1927	75.00	50.00
	L50	Scenes (1-50H) (F)	1927	60.00	40.00
	L50	Scenes (JCM1-50D) (F)	1927	60.00	40.00
	L50	Scenes (S1-S50) (F)	1928	60.00	40.00
	L50	Scenes (S51-S100) (F)	1928	60.00	40.00
	L50	Scenes (S100-S150) (F)	1928	60.00	40.00
	L4	Scenes (V1-4) (F)	1928	21.00	14.00
	28	Shots from the Films (F)	1938	66.00	44.00
73	M48	Sights of Britain 1st Series (F)	1936	15.00	10.00

Ref. No.	No. in Set	Name of Set	Date	COMPLETE SETS Grade 1	Grade 2
		J. A. PATTREIOUEX LTD. (Cont'd)			
74	M48	Sights of Britain 2nd Series (F)	1936	11.00	7.00
75	M48	Sights of Britain 3rd Series (F)	1937	11.00	7.00
1452	M48	Sights of London 1st Series (F)	1935	26.00	16.00
674	M12	Sights of London — Supplementary (F)	1935	15.00	7.50
	54	Sporting Celebrities (F)	1935	165.00	110.00
1454	M96	Sporting Events and Stars (F)	1935	125.00	75.00
	50	Sports Trophies	1931	150.00	100.00
76	M48	The Bridges of Britain (F)	1938	15.00	10.00
711	52	The English & Welsh Counties	1928	125.00	85.00
79	M48	The Navy (F)	1937	18.00	12.00
	M24	Treasure Island	1968	45.00	30.00
2493	51	Views (F)	1933	60.00	40.00
2929	54	Views of Britain (F)	1937	110.00	70.00
663	M48	Winter Scenes (F)	1937	15.00	10.00

		M. PEZARO & SON			
	25	Armies of the World	1899	4600.00	2300.00
	?25	Song Titles Illustrated	1900	6200.00	3100.00

		GODFREY PHILLIPS LTD.			
	50	Actresses (Oval, with maker's name)	1916	520.00	260.00
	50	Actresses (Oval without maker's name) A.A.	1916	420.00	210.00
	25	Actresses, C Series (Ball of Beauty Cigs.)	1900	4200.00	2100.00
	25	Actresses, C Series (Carriage Cigs.) A.A.	1900	1400.00	700.00
	25	Actresses, C Series (Derby Cigs.) A.A.	1900	3800.00	1900.00

COMPLETE SETS

Ref. No.	No. in Set	Name of Set	Date	Grade 1	Grade 2
		GODFREY PHILLIPS LTD. (Cont'd)			
	25	Actresses, C Series (Horseshoe back) A.A.	1900	1300.00	650.00
	25	Actresses, C Series (Teapot Cigs.) A.A.	1900	4200.00	2100.00
	25	Actresses, C Series (Volunteer Cigs.) A.A.	1900	4000.00	2000.00
	1	Advertisement Card (Grand Cut)	1934	14.00	9.00
	1	Advertisement Cards (La Calbana Fours)	1934	14.00	9.00
5590	50	Aircraft	1938	86.00	56.00
	54	Aircraft (Millhoff back)	1938	180.00	120.00
416	54	Aircraft Series No. 1 (Phillips back, matt front) A.A.	1938	34.00	20.00
	54	Aircraft Series No. 1 (Phillips back, varnished front) A.A.	1938	180.00	120.00
3282	40	Animal Series	1903	420.00	210.00
673	M30	Animal Studies	1936	16.00	8.00
	50	Animal Studies (Australia)	1930	90.00	60.00
632	50	Annuals	1939	15.00	10.00
716	50	Annuals (N.Z. planting dates) A.A.	1939	60.00	40.00
1788	L25	Arms of the English Sees	1924	135.00	90.00
	X32	Australian Birds (Carton Issue)	1968	11.00	7.00
	S16	Australian Gemstones (Carton Issue)	1970	9.00	6.00
	X24	Australian Scenes (Carton Issue)	1965	11.00	7.00
	50	Australian Sporting Celebrities	1932	135.00	90.00
	X32	Australian Wild Flowers (Carton Issue)	1967	11.00	7.00
	24	Beauties (HUMPS)	1899	3000.00	1500.00
3286	25	Beauties (Nd. B801-825)	1903	450.00	225.00
	30	Beauties, Nymphs	1897	3800.00	1900.00
5385	30	Beauties (Oval Plain Backs)	1914	110.00	55.00
	50	Beauties, Plums (Black & White)	1897	12000.00	6000.00
	50	Beauties, Plums (Green front) A.A.	1897	4400.00	2200.00
	50	Beauties, Plums (Plum front) A.A.	1897	4400.00	2200.00
2577	44	Beauties of Today	1937	75.00	50.00
1323	50	Beauties of Today 1st Series	1938	50.00	30.00
1324	36	Beauties of Today 2nd Series	1940	30.00	20.00
5248	54	Beauties of Today (F)	1939	90.00	60.00
3354	X36	Beauties of Today (Unnumbered) (F)	1937	72.00	48.00
2849	X36	Beauties of Today 2nd Series (F)	1938	60.00	40.00
2850	X36	Beauties of Today 3rd Series (F)	1938	45.00	30.00
3035	X36	Beauties of Today 4th Series (F)	1938	45.00	30.00
3036	X36	Beauties of Today 5th Series (F)	1938	30.00	20.00
3037	X36	Beauties of Today 6th Series (F)	1939	30.00	20.00
34	X36	Beauties of Today 7th Series (F)	1939	30.00	20.00

Ref. No.	No. in Set	Name of Set	Date	COMPLETE SETS Grade 1	Grade 2
		GODFREY PHILLIPS LTD. (Cont'd)			
29	X36	Beauties of Today (BVD back) (F)	1939	18.00	12.00
3365	36	Beauties of the World	1931	75.00	50.00
3360	36	Beauties of the World Series 2	1933	75.00	50.00
	50	Beautiful Women (I.F. Series)	1908	840.00	420.00
5383	50	Beautiful Women (W.I. Series) A.A.	1908	840.00	420.00
	L50	Beautiful Women (Nd. W501-W550)	1908	1600.00	800.00
819	P30	Beauty Spots of the Homeland	1938	9.00	6.00
205	50	Bird Painting	1938	24.00	14.00
	17	Boxers (B.V.D. Sports Package Issue)	1932	70.00	45.00
	25	Boxer Rebellion (Sketches)	1904	1000.00	500.00
	K76	British Beauties	1916	400.00	200.00
3855	54	British Beauties (1-54 Blue back) (F)	1914	230.00	115.00
	54	British Beauties (1-54 Plain back) (F) A.A.	1914	350.00	175.00
38	54	British Beauties (55-108 Blue back) (F)	1915	230.00	115.00
	54	British Beauties (55-108 Plain back) (F) A.A.	1915	320.00	160.00
	50	British Beauties (Photogravure)	1916	480.00	240.00
538	50	British Birds and Their Eggs	1936	56.00	36.00
1039	30	British Butterflies No. 1 Issue	1911	250.00	125.00
206	25	British Butterflies	1927	22.50	15.00
2091	25	British Butterflies (Transfers) A.A.	1936	18.00	12.00
1325	25	British Orders of Chivalry and Valour (De Reske Cigs.)	1939	39.00	26.00
717	25	British Orders of Chivalry & Valour (Phillips back) A.A.	1939	39.00	26.00
40	25	British Warships	1915	250.00	125.00
3154	L25	British Warships	1915	1600.00	800.00
	80	British Warships (F)	1916	1650.00	825.00
	50	Busts of Famous People (Brown back)	1906	1700.00	850.00
1878	50	Busts of Famous People (Green back) A.A.	1906	500.00	250.00
1187	M36	Characters Come to Life	1938	36.00	18.00
1670	25	Chinese Series (English Text back)	1910	240.00	120.00
850	25	Chinese Series (Volunteer Cigarettes back) A.A.	1910	300.00	150.00
2141	M25	Cinema Stars (Circular)	1924	120.00	60.00
3262	52	Cinema Stars (Set 1) (F)	1923	200.00	125.00
2752	30	Cinema Stars (Set 2 Brown)	1924	100.00	60.00
3285	30	Cinema Stars (Set 3 Black & White)	1925	60.00	40.00
2362	32	Cinema Stars (Set 4 Black & White)	1930	60.00	40.00
938	32	Cinema Stars (Set 5 Brown, Hand Coloured)	1934	55.00	35.00

Ref. No.	No. in Set	Name of Set	Date	COMPLETE SETS Grade 1	Grade 2
		GODFREY PHILLIPS LTD. (Cont'd)			
4039	30	Cinema Stars (Set 6 Plain back)	1935	26.00	16.00
	50	Colonial Troops	1904	2200.00	1100.00
461	50	Coronation of Their Majesties	1937	16.00	10.00
1188	M36	Coronation of Their Majesties I.A.	1937	12.00	8.00
41	P24	Coronation of Their Majesties I.A.	1937	40.00	26.00
	1	Cricket Fixture Card	1937	10.00	6.00
	55	Cricketers (B.D.V. Sports Package Issue)	1932	450.00	300.00
	25	Cricketers (Sports Package Issue)	1948	200.00	130.00
	25	Cricketers (Sports Package Issue)	1951	200.00	130.00
	K198	Cricketers (Pinnace) (F)	1924	2200.00	1100.00
941	?192	Cricketers (Brown back) (F)	1924	2600.00	1300.00
	L25	Cricketers (Brown back) (F)	1924	820.00	410.00
	L?75	Cricketers (Pinnace) (F)	1924	—	—
1327	25	Derby Winners & Jockeys	1923	140.00	70.00
1040	30	Eggs, Nests & Birds (Unnumbered)	1912	300.00	150.00
1041	30	Eggs, Nests & Birds (Numbered) A.A.	1913	270.00	135.00
1043	25	Empire Industries	1927	34.00	22.50
2299	49/50	Evolution of the British Navy	1930	75.00	45.00
1336	25	Famous Boys	1924	100.00	60.00
1337	32	Famous Cricketers	1926	230.00	130.00
207	25	Famous Crowns	1938	12.00	8.00
3854	50	Famous Footballers	1936	80.00	50.00
255	M36	Famous Love Scenes	1939	24.00	16.00
94	50	Famous Minors	1936	16.00	10.00
3880	P26	Famous Paintings	1938	48.00	28.00
1564	25	Feathered Friends	1928	50.00	30.00
146	50	Film Favourites	1934	25.00	15.00
455	50	Film Stars	1934	25.00	15.00
	50	Film Stars (Australian Issue)	1934	90.00	60.00
	67	Film Stars (B.D.V. Package Issue)	1932	120.00	80.00
2825	P24	Film Stars (Series of 24 Postcard back)	1934	66.00	36.00
	P24	Film Stars (Series of 24 Non-Postcard back) A.A.	1934	100.00	60.00
	P24	Film Stars (Series of cards, Postcard back)	1934	48.00	32.00
	P24	Film Stars (Series of cards, Non-Postcard back) A.A.	1934	100.00	60.00
5617	P24	Film Stars 2nd Series (25-48 Postcard back)	1934	120.00	70.00
	P24	Film Stars (25-48 Non-Postcard back) A.A.	1934	160.00	90.00
2392	25	First Aid Series	1914	260.00	130.00
1326	50	First Aid	1923	80.00	50.00
3296	25	Fish	1924	80.00	50.00

A SELECTION OF NATURAL HISTORY SETS

SET 1140

SET 1141

PLAYERS SET 827

SET 307

B.A.T. (A.A. SET 827)

WILLS SET 1210

GODREY PHILLIPS
SET 673

SET 405

Ref. No.	No. in Set	Name of Set	Date	COMPLETE SETS Grade 1	Grade 2
		GODFREY PHILLIPS LTD. (Cont'd)			
574	M30	Flower Studies	1937	10.25	6.25
2933	M30	Flower Studies A.A.	1937	15.00	9.00
		Footballers Miniature size "Pinance" photos issues	1922-24		
1621	K112	Brown Oval Design Back (F)		500.00	300.00
1622	K400	Black Oval Design Back (F)		680.00	420.00
1619	K517	Oblong Double Lined Back (F)		1200.00	700.00
1620	K1109	Oblong Single Lined Back (F)		—	—
1623	K2463	Front Name at Top, Team at Base (F)		—	—
1625	K?200	Front Team at Top, Name at Base (F)		420.00	260.00
	132	Footballers (B.D.V. Sports Package Issue)	1932	390.00	260.00
	25	Footballers (Sports Package Issue)	1948	110.00	70.00
	50	Footballers (Sports Package Issue)	1950	210.00	140.00
	25	Footballers (Sports Package Issue)	1951	105.00	70.00
	25	Footballers & Rugby Players (Sports Package Issue)	1952	105.00	70.00
42	P30	Garden Studies	1938	11.00	7.00
	13	General Interest	1899	1020.00	510.00
	?100	Guinea Gold Series Actresses (Brown)	1900	1500.00	750.00
	160	Guinea Gold Series (Black & White)	1900	1050.00	525.00
	90	Guinea Gold Series (Numbered 101-190)	1900	620.00	310.00
	100	Guinea Gold Series	1900	850.00	425.00
1332	25	Home Pets	1924	60.00	40.00
1826	25	How to Build a 2 Valve Set	1929	80.00	50.00
5560	25	How to Do It Series	1913	300.00	150.00
1329	25	How to Make a Valve Amplifier	1924	80.00	50.00
1328	25	How to Make Your Own Wireless Set	1923	70.00	40.00
1842	25	Indian Series	1908	640.00	320.00
524	54	In the Public Eye	1935	25.00	15.00
653	50	International Caps	1936	70.00	40.00
	52	Jig-Saw Inserts	1933	—	—
	19	Jockeys (B.D.V. Sports Package Issue)	1932	60.00	40.00
	25	Jockeys (Sports Package Issue)	1952	100.00	66.00
	37	Kings & Queens of England	1925	200.00	110.00
2895	35/37	Kings & Queens of England A.A.	1925	100.00	60.00
1331	25	Lawn Tennis	1903	80.00	50.00
	K53	Miniature Playing Cards (Blue, scroll back)	1933	40.00	25.00
	K53	Miniature Playing Cards (Buff)	1932	40.00	25.00
	K52	Miniature Playing Cards (Red back)	1906	—	—

SET No: 653

SET No: 418

SET No: 1046

SET No: 542

SET No: 1836

SET No: 3982

SET No: 1330

SET No: 1045

Ref. No.	No. in Set	Name of Set	Date	Grade 1	Grade 2
		COMPLETE SETS			
		GODFREY PHILLIPS LTD. (Cont'd)			
	K53	Miniature Playing Cards (White, red overprinting)	1934	50.00	30.00
	K53	Miniature Playing Cards (Yellow)	1933	50.00	30.00
2756	25	Model Railways	1927	100.00	60.00
	30	Morse & Semaphore Signalling (Morse back)	1916	360.00	180.00
	30	Morse & Semaphore Signalling (Semaphore back) A.A.	1916	360.00	180.00
1044	50	Motor Cars at a Glance	1924	280.00	140.00
	20	Novelty Series	1924	300.00	150.00
3982	25	Old Favourites	1924	60.00	30.00
256	M36	Old Masters	1939	18.00	11.00
1330	36	Olympic Champions Amsterdam	1928	70.00	40.00
1046	25	Optical Illusions	1927	70.00	40.00
1045	36	Our Dogs	1939	70.00	40.00
243	M30	Our Dogs A.A.	1939	28.00	14.00
2898	P30	Our Dogs A.A.	1939	200.00	100.00
274	M48	Our Favourites	1935	18.00	9.00
820	P30	Our Glorious Empire	1939	16.00	9.00
1190	M30	Our Puppies	1936	22.00	11.00
2899	P30	Our Puppies A.A.	1936	80.00	40.00
1047	25	Personalities of Today (Caricatures)	1932	70.00	35.00
1338	25	Popular Superstitions	1930	50.00	30.00
	X20	Private Seal Wrestling Holds	1930	—	—
2272	25	Prizes for Needlework	1925	75.00	45.00
	25	Radio Stars (Package Issue)	1949	75.00	50.00
418	25	Railway Engines	1934	100.00	60.00
	K27	Real Photo Series (War Leaders Cut-Outs) (F)	1916	320.00	160.00
12	25	Red Indians	1927	100.00	55.00
	20	Russo Japanese War Series	1905	—	—
1239	25	School Badges	1927	40.00	24.00
482	48	Screen Stars (Series A, Embossed)	1936	70.00	40.00
760	48	Screen Stars (Series A, Not Embossed) A.A.	1936	120.00	60.00
761	48	Screen Stars (Series B) (Different)	1936	70.00	40.00
3295	48	Selection of B.D.V. Wonderful Gifts	1930	80.00	40.00
1334	48	Selection of B.D.V. Wonderful Gifts	1931	80.00	40.00
1333	48	Selection of B.D.V. Wonderful Gifts	1932	80.00	40.00
1335	25	Ships and Their Flags	1924	120.00	60.00
	X32	Sea Life on the Great Barrier Reef (Carton issue)	1968	7.50	5.00

Ref. No.	No. in Set	Name of Set	Date	COMPLETE SETS Grade 1	Grade 2
		GODFREY PHILLIPS LTD. (Cont'd)			
253	M36	Ships that have Made History	1938	18.00	9.00
254	M48	Shots from the Films	1934	30.00	15.00
1339	50	Soccer Stars	1936	80.00	40.00
258	36	Soldiers of the King	1939	36.00	18.00
1191	M20	Special Jubilee Year Series	1935	10.00	6.00
43	P12	Special Jubilee Year Series A.A.	1935	40.00	20.00
1448	30	Speed Champions	1930	70.00	40.00
	21	Speedway Riders (B.D.V. Sports Package Issue)	1932	180.00	120.00
1048	36	Sporting Champions	1929	75.00	45.00
43	25	Sporting Series	1909	760.00	380.00
3497	25	Sports	1923	150.00	75.00
	28	Sportsmen (B.D.V. Sports Package Issue)	1932	90.00	60.00
	50	Sportsmen (Sports Package Issue)	1948	165.00	110.00
	25	Sportsmen (Sports Package Issue)	1949	90.00	60.00
	25	Sportsmen (Sports Package Issue)	1953	90.00	60.00
	25	Sportsmen (Sports Package Issue)	1954	90.00	60.00
1049	50	Sportsmen — Spot the Winner (Back Inverted)	1937	40.00	20.00
762	50	Sportsmen — Spot the Winner (Back Normal) A.A.	1937	50.00	25.00
4021	35	Stage and Cinema Beauties (Series A)	1933	55.00	35.00
	35	Stage & Cinema Beauties (Series B) (Different)	1933	50.00	30.00
3271	50	Stage & Cinema Beauties	1935	80.00	50.00
763	1	Stamp Cards (real stamp affixed)	1928	2.00	1.00
5561	50	Stars of British Films (B.D.V. Aust.)	1934	140.00	70.00
	50	Stars of British Films (De Reske, Aust.) A.A.	1934	140.00	70.00
	50	Stars of British Films (Godfrey Phillips, Aust.) A.A.	1934	140.00	70.00
	50	Stars of British Films (Grey's Aust.) A.A.	1934	140.00	70.00
1342	54	Stars of the Screen	1934	120.00	60.00
257	48	Stars of the Screen (Embossed) (Different)	1936	45.00	25.00
764	48	Stars of the Screen (Not Embossed) A.A.	1936	45.00	25.00
1877	25	Statues & Monuments (Cut-Outs) (Pat. No. 20736)	1907	300.00	150.00
	25	Statues & Monuments (Cut-Outs) (Prov. Pat. No. 20736) A.A.	1907	300.00	150.00

COMPLETE SETS

Ref. No.	No. in Set	Name of Set	Date	Grade 1	Grade 2
		GODFREY PHILLIPS LTD. (Cont'd)			
840	25	Territorial Series (Nd. 51-75)	1908	920.00	460.00
2274	38	Test Cricketers (Australia) (B.D.V. Cigarettes)	1932	140.00	70.00
	38	Test Cricketers (Australia) (Grey's Cigarettes) A.A.	1932	140.00	70.00
	38	Test Cricketers (Australia) (Godfrey Phillips back) A.A.	1933	140.00	70.00
3853	25	The 1924 Cabinet	1924	60.00	40.00
417	48	The Old Country	1935	44.00	24.00
586	50	This Mechanized Age 1st Series (Adhesive)	1936	15.00	10.00
843	50	This Mechanized Age 1st Series (Non-adhesive) A.A.	1936	25.00	15.00
259	50	This Mechanized Age 2nd Series	1937	18.00	12.00
	25	Types of British & Colonial Troops	1900	1900.00	950.00
	25	Types of British Soldiers (No. M651-675)	1900	800.00	400.00
	75	Victorian Footballers (Australia)	1933	150.00	100.00
	50	Victorian Footballers (Australia) (Godfrey Phillips)	1933	120.00	80.00
	50	Victorian Footballers (Australia) (B.D.V. Cigarettes) A.A.	1933	120.00	80.00
	50	Victorian Footballers (Australia) (Grey's Cigarettes) A.A.	1933	120.00	80.00
	50	Victorian League & Association Footballers	1934	140.00	90.00
	63	War Photos (F)	1916	850.00	425.00
	100	Who's Who in Australian Sport	1933	240.00	160.00
4041	X30	Zoo Studies (ST)	1939	48.00	24.00
726	1	Zoo Studies (3D Spectacles)	1939	8.00	4.00

GODFREY PHILLIPS LTD. (SILK ISSUES)
Issued about 1910-1925

M62	Arms of Countries & Territories		400.00	200.00
B32	Beauties — Modern Paintings		660.00	330.00
P32	Beauties — Modern Paintings A.A.		—	—
B100	Birds		450.00	225.00
M12	Birds of the Tropics		250.00	125.00
L12	Birds of the Tropics A.A.		300.00	150.00
P12	Birds of the Tropics A.A.		400.00	200.00
X24	British Admirals		230.00	115.00

Ref. No.	No. in Set	Name of Set	Date	COMPLETE SETS Grade 1	Grade 2

GODFREY PHILLIPS LTD. (SILK ISSUES) (Cont'd)
Issued about 1910-1925

Ref. No.	No. in Set	Name of Set	Grade 1	Grade 2
	M & L50	British Butterflies & Moths	300.00	150.00
	M108	British Naval Crests (Anonymous)	280.00	140.00
	M108	British Naval Crests (B.D.V.) A.A.	320.00	160.00
	L25	Butterflies	440.00	220.00
365	M47	Ceramic Art	100.00	50.00
	L47	Ceramic Art A.A.	160.00	80.00
718	B65	Clan Tartans (B.D.V.)	130.00	65.00
	M65	Clan Tartans A.A.	110.00	55.00
	M49	Clan Tartans (Anonymous) A.A.	100.00	50.00
	P12	Clan Tartans (12 from set 718)	110.00	55.00
	M108	Colonial Army Badges	280.00	140.00
	M17	County Cricket Badges (Anonymous)	420.00	210.00
	M17	County Cricket Badges (B.D.V.) A.A.	420.00	210.00
3938	M108	Crests & Badges of the British Army (Anonymous)	160.00	80.00
	M108	Crests & Badges of the British Army (B.D.V.) A.A.	160.00	80.00
	L108	Crests & Badges of the British Army (Anonymous) A.A.	260.00	130.00
	L108	Crests & Badges of the British Army (B.D.V.) A.A.	280.00	140.00
	M143	Flags (Set 4)	200.00	100.00
	M24	Flags (Set 5)	44.00	22.00
	M18	Flags (Set 6)	30.00	15.00
4022	M20	Flags (Set 7)	36.00	18.00
	M50	Flags (5th Series)	140.00	70.00
	M120	Flags (7th Series)	160.00	80.00
	L120	Flags (10th Series)	180.00	90.00
	M120	Flags (12th Series)	160.00	80.00
	M132	Flags (20th Series)	170.00	85.00
	M126	Flags (25th Series)	160.00	80.00
	L120	Flags (26th Series)	160.00	80.00
	M?90	Football Colours	—	—
	P?90	Football Colours	680.00	340.00
	M126	G.P. Territorial Badges	340.00	170.00
894	L25	Great War Leaders (Sepia)	240.00	120.00
	S47	Great War Leaders & Celebrities	300.00	150.00
	M51	Great War Leaders & Warships	520.00	260.00
	B25	Heraldic Series	50.00	25.00
3289	M25	Heraldic Series A.A.	50.00	25.00
	L25	Heraldic Series A.A.	130.00	65.00

				COMPLETE SETS	
Ref. No.	No. in Set	Name of Set	Date	Grade 1	Grade 2

GODFREY PHILLIPS LTD. (SILK ISSUES) (Cont'd)
Issued about 1910-1925

Ref. No.	No. in Set	Name of Set	Date	Grade 1	Grade 2
2596	P12	Heraldic Series A.A.		100.00	50.00
	M26	House Flags		320.00	160.00
	M10	Irish Patriots		220.00	110.00
	X10	Irish Patriots A.A.		220.00	110.00
	P10	Irish Patriots A.A.		320.00	160.00
2908	M1	Irish Republican Stamp		3.50	1.75
	M54	Naval Badges of Rank & Military Headdress		550.00	275.00
	S1	Nelson's Signal at Trafalgar		80.00	40.00
	S40	Old Masters (Set 1)		2200.00	1100.00
	S20	Old Masters (Set 2) (Anonymous)		170.00	85.00
	S20	Old Masters (Set 2) (B.D.V.) A.A.		150.00	75.00
	M40	Old Masters (Set 3)		200.00	100.00
	M120	Old Masters (Set 4)		400.00	200.00
3348	M60	Old Masters (Set 5)		160.00	80.00
3011	B50	Old Masters (Set 6)		150.00	75.00
	M50	Old Masters (Set 7) Nd. 301-350		220.00	110.00
	M50	Orders of Chivalry		200.00	100.00
3294	M24	Orders of Chivalry (B.D.V. 1-24)		70.00	35.00
	M24	Orders of Chivalry (GP 401-424) A.A.		90.00	45.00
	M25	Pilot & Signal Flags (Anonymous, No. 601-625)		100.00	50.00
	M25	Pilot & Signal Flags (B.D.V.) A.A.		80.00	40.00
	L72	Regimental Colours		550.00	275.00
	M50	Regimental Colours, Series 12		170.00	85.00
	M120	Regimental Colours & Crests (Anonymous)		230.00	115.00
	M120	Regimental Colours & Crests (B.D.V.) A.A.		230.00	115.00
	S120	Regimental Colours & Crests (Anonymous, Un Nd.) A.A.		1000.00	500.00
	S120	Regimental Colours & Crests (B.D.V. No.) A.A.		1000.00	500.00
	M10	Religious Pictures		320.00	160.00
	X10	Religious Pictures A.A.		320.00	160.00
	S10	Religious Pictures A.A.		520.00	260.00
3311	B1	The Allies Flags (Four Flags)		17.00	8.50
	S1	The Allies Flags (Four Flags)		18.00	9.00
2600	S1	The Allies Flags (Seven Flags)		17.00	8.50
3310	S1	The Allies Flags (Eight Flags)		50.00	25.00
	M75	Town & City Arms		260.00	130.00

Ref. No.	No. in Set	Name of Set	Date	COMPLETE SETS Grade 1	Grade 2

GODFREY PHILLIPS LTD. (SILK ISSUES) (Cont'd)
Issued about 1910-1925

	L75	Town & City Arms		260.00	130.00
	M25	Victoria Cross Heroes I		450.00	225.00
	M24	Victoria Cross Heroes II (with Flags)		520.00	260.00
	M90	War Pictures		950.00	475.00

PIZZUTO (MALTA)

| | 50 | Milton's Paradise Lost | 1910 | 350.00 | 175.00 |

THE PLANTERS STORES & AGENCY CO. LTD. (INDIA)

| | 50 | Actesses "FROGA" | 1900 | 2300.00 | 1150.00 |
| | 25 | Beauties "FECKSA" (Plum Coloured) | 1900 | 1300.00 | 650.00 |

JOHN PLAYER & SONS

Ref. No.	No. in Set	Name of Set	Date	Grade 1	Grade 2
3120	25	Actors & Actresses	1898	1200.00	600.00
	50	Actresses	1898	2250.00	1125.00
	8	Advertisement Cards	1894	—	—
	1	Advertisement Card (Grosvenor Cigarettes)	1970	1.50	1.00
851	1	Advertisement Card (Sailor)	1929	8.00	4.00
821	L1	Advertisement Card (Sailor) A.A.	1929	40.00	20.00
5637	1	Advertisement Card (Wants List)	1936	2.00	1.00
	50	Aeroplane Series (Overseas, Gilt border)	1926	170.00	85.00
47	50	Aeroplanes (Civil)	1935	64.00	32.00
1037	50	Aeroplanes (Irish Issue) A.A.	1935	95.00	55.00
4	50	Aircraft of the Royal Air Force	1938	70.00	35.00
	50	Aircraft of the Royal Air Force (Overseas, no I.T.C.) A.A.	1938	90.00	45.00
140	X10	Allied Cavalry (Also issued as Regimental Uniforms)	1914	140.00	70.00
1113	L24	A Nature Calendar	1930	144.00	72.00
60	50	Animals of the Countryside	1939	22.00	11.00
	50	Animals of the Countryside (Irish Issue) A.A.	1939	80.00	40.00

COMPLETE SETS

Ref. No.	No. in Set	Name of Set	Date	Grade 1	Grade 2
		JOHN PLAYER & SONS (Cont'd)			
790	50	Animals of the Countryside (Overseas, no I.T.C.) A.A.	1939	60.00	30.00
1114	L25	Aquarium Studies	1932	75.00	45.00
319	L25	Architectural Beauties	1927	78.00	48.00
295	50	Arms & Armour (Blue back)	1909	270.00	135.00
	50	Arms & Armour (Grey back) (Overseas, no I.T.C.) A.A.	1926	215.00	125.00
187	50	Army Corps & Divisional Signs 1st	1924	20.00	10.00
366	100	Army Corps & Divisional Signs 2nd	1925	50.00	25.00
133	25	Army Life	1910	70.00	35.00
346	X12	Artillery in Action	1917	90.00	45.00
	50	A Sectional Map of Ireland	1933	140.00	90.00
186	50	Association Cup Winners	1930	120.00	60.00
93	50	Aviary and Cage Birds	1933	76.00	38.00
1374	50	Aviary and Cage Birds (Transfers) A.A.	1933	18.00	10.00
1308	L25	Aviary and Cage Birds A.A.	1935	120.00	60.00
1026	50	Badges & Flags of British Regiments (Brown back, Numbered)	1904	170.00	85.00
1027	50	Badges & Flags of British Regiments (Brown back, Unnumbered) A.A.	1904	240.00	120.00
1363	50	Badges & Flags of British Regiments (Green back)	1904	180.00	90.00
	P9	Basket Ball Fixtures	1972	—	—
	50	Beauties (Overseas) (F)	1925	110.00	55.00
	B50	Beauties (Coloured — Overseas) (F)	1925	140.00	70.00
	50	Beauties 2nd Series (Overseas) (F)	1925	110.00	55.00
177	50	Birds & Their Young	1937	22.00	12.00
	50	Birds & Their Young (Overseas, no I.T.C.) A.A.	1937	48.00	28.00
	50	Birds & Their Young (Irish, adhesive) A.A.	1937	72.00	36.00
	50	Birds & Their Young (Irish, Non-adhesive) A.A.	1937	90.00	45.00
286	25	Birds & Their Young 1st Series (Non-adhesive) (As set 177)	Unissued	6.00	4.00
269	25	Birds & Their Young 2nd Series (Non-adhesive) (As set 177)	Unissued	6.00	4.00
	52	Birds of Brilliant Plumage (Overseas, P/C Inset)	1927	280.00	160.00
	25	"Bonzo" Dogs (Overseas)	1923	160.00	80.00
	P10	Bookmarks (Authors) (F)	1900	1050.00	525.00
1029	25	Boxing (Irish)	1934	200.00	100.00

SET No: 138

SET No: 366

SET No: 295

SET No: 1026

SET No: 60

SET No: 296

SET No: 177

SET No: 186

SET No: 93

**COMPLETE
SETS**

Ref. No.	No. in Set	Name of Set	Date	Grade 1	Grade 2
		JOHN PLAYER & SONS (Cont'd)			
	30	Boy Scouts (Overseas)	1924	180.00	90.00
138	50	Boy Scout & Girl Guide Signs	1933	28.00	14.00
1376	50	Boy Scout & Girl Guide Signs (Transfers)	1933	16.00	10.00
1634	D32	Britain's Endangered Wildlife (Doncella)	1984	5.25	—
1602	D32	Britain's Endangered Wildlife (Grandee)	1984	7.00	—
1635	D30	Britain's Wild Flowers (Doncella)	1986	5.75	—
1603	D30	Britain's Wild Flowers (Grandee)	1986	7.50	—
85	D32	British Birds (Grandee Cigars)	1980	12.00	—
1117	L25	British Butterflies	1934	150.00	75.00
719	D32	British Butterflies (Doncella)	1984	6.50	—
720	D32	British Butterflies (Grandee) A.A.	1983	7.50	—
296	50	British Empire Series	1904	110.00	55.00
367	25	British Livestock	1915	64.00	32.00
1116	X25	British Livestock (Blue back) A.A.	1923	80.00	40.00
1727	X25	British Livestock (Brown back) A.A.	1916	110.00	55.00
	X25	British Livestock (Overseas, no I.T.C.) A.A.	1924	250.00	125.00
721	D30	British Mammals (Doncella)	1983	5.50	—
722	D30	British Mammals (Grandee) A.A.	1983	6.25	—
576	L25	British Naval Craft	1939	28.00	14.00
1567	X20	British Pedigree Stock	1925	80.00	40.00
1115	L25	British Regalia	1937	48.00	26.00
188	50	Butterflies	1932	100.00	50.00
1372	50	Butterflies (Transfers) A.A.	1932	16.00	10.00
831	50	Butterflies (Girls) (Overseas)	1928	450.00	225.00
1031	50	Butterflies and Moths	1904	170.00	85.00
645	25	Bygone Beauties	1914	60.00	30.00
1118	X10	Bygone Beauties A.A.	1916	90.00	45.00
	?S30	Cabinet Size Pictures	1898	4500.00	2250.00
5594	20	Castles, Abbeys etc. (No border)	1894	1200.00	600.00
828	20	Castles Abbeys etc. (White border) A.A.	1894	1000.00	500.00
1119	L24	Cats	1936	300.00	150.00
1032	50	Celebrated Bridges	1903	230.00	115.00
347	50	Celebrated Gateways	1909	110.00	55.00
131	25	Ceremonial and Court Dress	1911	90.00	45.00
1120	L25	Championship Golf Courses	1936	280.00	140.00
620	25	Characters from Dickens 1st Series	1912	100.00	50.00
297	25	Characters from Dickens 2nd Series	1914	100.00	50.00
1121	X10	Characters from Dickens	1912	120.00	60.00

A SELECTION FROM PLAYER'S

SET No: 347

SET No: 51

SET No: 249

SET No: 2

SET No: 299

SET No: 309

SET No: 136

SET No: 226

Ref. No.	No. in Set	Name of Set	Date	COMPLETE SETS Grade 1	Grade 2

JOHN PLAYER & SONS (Cont'd)

Ref. No.	No. in Set	Name of Set	Date	Grade 1	Grade 2
88	50	Characters from Dickens (Reissued)	1923	140.00	70.00
326	L25	Characters from Fiction	1933	130.00	65.00
298	25	Characters from Thackeray	1913	70.00	35.00
1674	50	Cities of the World	1900	330.00	165.00
	50	Civil Aircraft	Unissued	—	—
1569	L20	Clocks — Old and New	1928	185.00	95.00
299	25	Colonial & Indian Army Badges	1916	50.00	25.00
26	50	Coronation Series — Ceremonial Dress	1937	24.00	12.00
	50	Coronation Series Ceremonial Dress (Overseas, no I.T.C.) A.A.	1937	50.00	25.00
249	25	Countries and Their Industries (Numbered)	1914	56.00	28.00
250	25	Countries and Their Industries (Unnumbered) A.A.	1911	56.00	28.00
412	50	Countries Arms & Flags	1905	64.00	32.00
80	D32	Country Houses and Castles (Doncella Cigars)	1981	5.00	—
309	50	Country Seats and Arms 1st Series	1906	70.00	35.00
310	50	Country Seats and Arms 2nd Series	1907	70.00	35.00
1365	50	Country Seats and Arms 3rd Series	1907	70.00	35.00
327	L25	Country Sports	1930	190.00	95.00
348	50	Cricketers	1930	112.00	56.00
90	50	Cricketers 1934	1934	70.00	35.00
179	50	Cricketers 1938	1938	56.00	28.00
	50	Cricketers 1938 (Overseas, no I.T.C.) A.A.	1938	120.00	60.00
349	50	Cricketers Caricatures by RIP	1926	140.00	70.00
242	25	Cries of London 1st Series	1913	100.00	50.00
1726	X10	Cries of London 1st Series A.A.	1912	96.00	48.00
51	25	Cries of London 2nd Series	1916	50.00	25.00
1122	X10	Cries of London 2nd Series A.A.	1914	70.00	35.00
	25	Cries of London 2nd Series (Black back) A.A.	Unissued	—	—
241	50	Curious Beaks	1929	24.00	12.00
2	50	Cycling	1939	60.00	30.00
	50	Cycling (Irish Issue — adhesive) A.A.	1939	80.00	40.00
	50	Cycling (Irish Issue — non-adhesive) A.A.	1939	90.00	45.00
	50	Cycling (Overseas, no I.T.C.) A.A.	1939	60.00	30.00
226	50	Dandies	1932	28.00	14.00
1123	L25	Dandies A.A.	1932	90.00	45.00
1407	50	Decorations & Medals	Unissued	100.00	—

Ref. No.	No. in Set	Name of Set	Date	COMPLETE SETS Grade 1	Grade 2
		JOHN PLAYER & SONS (Cont'd)			
136	50	Derby & Grand National Winners	1933	160.00	80.00
1373	50	Derby & Grand National Winners (Transfers) A.A.	1933	30.00	15.00
368	50	Dogs (Scenic background)	1925	80.00	40.00
1126	X12	Dogs (Scenic background) A.A.	1924	60.00	30.00
287	50	Dogs Heads by Beigel	Unissued	30.00	18.00
139	50	Dogs Heads by Wardle	1929	80.00	40.00
	25	Dogs Heads (Irish Issue) A.A.	1927	84.00	42.00
3801	25	Dogs Heads (Irish Issue 2nd Series)	1929	84.00	42.00
1124	L20	Dogs Heads by Wardle	1926	84.00	42.00
1125	L20	Dogs Heads by Wardle (2nd Series)	1928	80.00	40.00
	25	Dogs (Heads) (Overseas)	1927	48.00	24.00
125	50	Dogs by Wardle (Full Length)	1931	64.00	32.00
1370	50	Dogs by Wardle (Full Length Transfers) A.A.	1931	16.00	10.00
1887	L25	Dogs by Wardle (Full Length) A.A.	1933	104.00	52.00
3819	50	Dogs Heads (Silver Grey Background)	1940	280.00	140.00
2194	L25	Dogs (Pairs and Groups)	Unissued	48.00	24.00
189	50	Drum Banners & Cap Badges	1924	64.00	32.00
	32	Drum Horses (Overseas)	1911	360.00	180.00
300	25	Egyptian Kings & Queens and Classical Deities	1911	60.00	30.00
3143	X10	Egyptian Sketches	1915	76.00	38.00
	25	England's Military Heroes	1898	1900.00	950.00
	25	England's Military Heroes (Plain back) A.A.	1898	1500.00	750.00
3115	25	England's Military Heroes (Narrow card) A.A.	1899	1370.00	685.00
	25	England's Military Heroes (Narrow card — Plain back) A.A.	1899	1250.00	625.00
943	25	England's Naval Heroes (without descriptions on back)	1897	1720.00	860.00
3886	25	England's Naval Heroes (without descriptions on back — Narrow card) A.A.	1897	1100.00	550.00
	25	England's Naval Heroes (with descriptions on back)	1899	1750.00	875.00
1550	25	England's Naval Heroes (Narrow card) A.A.	1899	1120.00	560.00
	25	England's Naval Heroes (Plain back) A.A.	1898	1050.00	525.00

Ref. No.	No. in Set	Name of Set	Date	COMPLETE SETS Grade 1	Grade 2
		JOHN PLAYER & SONS (Cont'd)			
1551	25	England's Naval Heroes (Plain back Narrow card) A.A.	1898	900.00	450.00
2259	25	Everyday Phrases by Tom Browne	1901	650.00	325.00
732	L32	Exploration of Space (Tom Thumb Cigars)	1982	7.00	—
1129	L25	Fables by Aesop	1927	120.00	60.00
830	20	Famous Authors and Poets	1902	1040.00	520.00
3130	20	Famous Authors and Poets (Narrow card) A.A.	1903	750.00	375.00
267	L25	Famous Beauties	1937	70.00	40.00
	L25	Famous Beauties (Overseas, no I.T.C.) A.A.	1937	70.00	40.00
805	50	Famous Irish-Bred Horses	1936	260.00	130.00
806	50	Famous Irish Greyhounds	1935	360.00	180.00
86	D28	Famous M.G. Marques (Grandee Cigar)	1981	12.00	—
1130	X10	Famous Paintings	1913	60.00	30.00
49	50	Film Stars 1st Series	1934	100.00	50.00
192	50	Film Stars 2nd Series	1934	70.00	35.00
	50	Film Stars 2nd Series (Irish Issue) A.A.	1934	140.00	70.00
25	50	Film Stars 3rd Series	1938	60.00	30.00
	50	Film Stars 3rd Series (Overseas, no I.T.C.) A.A.	1938	84.00	42.00
1131	L25	Film Stars	1934	120.00	60.00
	L25	Film Stars (Irish Issue) A.A.	1934	270.00	135.00
493	50	Fire Fighting Appliances	1930	140.00	70.00
1366	50	Fishes of the World	1903	160.00	80.00
	25	Flag Girls of All Nations (Overseas)	1908	270.00	135.00
92	50	Flags of the League of Nations	1928	28.00	14.00
407	50	Football Caricatures by 'Mac'	1927	70.00	35.00
301	50	Footballers Caricatures by 'Rip'	1926	70.00	35.00
511	50	Footballers 1928	1928	70.00	35.00
604	25	Footballers 1928-9 2nd Series	1929	30.00	15.00
1025	50	Freshwater Fishes (White back)	1934	110.00	55.00
197	50	Freshwater Fishes (Pink back) A.A.	1933	70.00	35.00
1132	L25	Freshwater Fishes A.A.	1935	110.00	55.00
2417	L25	Freshwater Fishes (Non-adhesive Irish Issue) A.A.	1935	260.00	130.00
408	25	From Plantation to Smoker	1926	10.00	6.00
	50	Gallery of Beauty Series	1897	2400.00	1200.00
	50	Gallery of Beauty (Narrow card) A.A.	1897	1700.00	850.00
	5	Gallery of Beauty 5 different cards	1897	—	—
	5	Gallery of Beauty (Narrow) A.A.	1897	—	—

A SELECTION FROM PLAYER'S

SET No: 511

SET No: 25

SET No: 407

SET No: 125

SET No: 300

SET No: 92

SET No: 493

SET No: 49

Ref. No.	No. in Set	Name of Set	Date	COMPLETE SETS Grade 1	Grade 2
		JOHN PLAYER & SONS (Cont'd)			
409	50	Game Birds & Wild Fowl	1927	104.00	52.00
1128	L25	Game Birds & Wild Fowl A.A.	1928	160.00	80.00
239	25	Gems of British Scenery	1914	32.00	16.00
190	50	Gilbert & Sullivan	1925	100.00	50.00
1127	X25	Gilbert & Sullivan A.A.	1926	130.00	65.00
89	50	Gilbert & Sullivan 2nd Series	1925	90.00	45.00
1568	L25	Gilbert & Sullivan 2nd Series A.A.	1926	130.00	65.00
322	L25	Golf	1939	390.00	195.00
724	L25	Golf (Overseas, no I.T.C.) A.A.	1939	360.00	180.00
527	25	Hidden Beauties	1929	8.50	5.50
130	25	Highland Clans	1908	120.00	60.00
48	50	Hints on Association Football	1934	48.00	24.00
1660	X10	Historic Ships	1910	84.00	42.00
1606	L30	History of Motor Racing (Tom Thumb)	1986	10.00	—
240	50	History of Naval Dress	1930	80.00	40.00
324	L25	History of Naval Dress A.A.	1929	90.00	45.00
81	D24	History of the V.C. (Doncella Cigars)	1980	15.00	—
82	D1	History of the V.C. (Completion Offer) (Doncella Cigars)	1981	3.00	—
	50	Household Hints (Overseas)	1928	70.00	40.00
59	50	International Air Liners	1936	32.00	16.00
	50	International Air Liners (Irish Issue) A.A.	1936	72.00	36.00
	50	International Air Liners (Overseas — adhesive) A.A.	1936	56.00	28.00
	50	International Air Liners (Overseas — non-adhesive) A.A.	1936	72.00	36.00
2258	25	Irish Place Names	1927	90.00	45.00
1615	25	Irish Place Names 2nd Series	1929	90.00	45.00
	M5	Jubilee Issue	1960	6.00	—
182	50	Kings & Queens of England	1935	96.00	48.00
1133	L50	Kings & Queens of England A.A.	1935	220.00	110.00
	50	Lawn Tennis (Overseas)	1928	165.00	85.00
	50	Leaders of Men (Overseas)	1925	150.00	75.00
302	50	Life on Board a Man of War	1905	180.00	90.00
	D7	Limericks (Panama)	1977	45.00	30.00
44	25	Live Stock	1925	115.00	65.00
410	50	Military Headdress	1931	84.00	42.00
1378	50	Military Series	1900	1800.00	900.00
180	50	Military Uniforms of the British Empire Overseas	1938	60.00	30.00

SET No: 180

SET No: 190

SET No: 89

SET No: 181

SET No: 527

SET No: 410

SET No; 409

SET No: 240

Ref. No.	No. in Set	Name of Set	Date	Grade 1	Grade 2
		COMPLETE SETS			
		JOHN PLAYER & SONS (Cont'd)			
	50	Military Uniforms of the British Empire (Overseas — adhesive) A.A.	1938	90.00	45.00
829	50	Military Uniforms of the British Empire (Overseas non-adhesive) A.A.	1938	120.00	60.00
91	25	Miniatures	1923	16.00	8.00
178	50	Modern Naval Craft	1939	40.00	20.00
	50	Modern Naval Craft (Irish Issue) A.A.	1939	80.00	40.00
	50	Modern Naval Craft (Overseas, no I.T.C.) A.A.	1939	64.00	32.00
57	50	Motor Cars 1st Series	1936	110.00	55.00
	50	Motor Cars A Series (Overseas, no I.T.C.) A.A.	1936	140.00	70.00
	50	Motor Cars (Irish Issue) A.A.	1936	150.00	75.00
181	50	Motor Cars 2nd Series	1937	84.00	42.00
	50	Motor Cars 2nd Series (Overseas, no I.T.C.) A.A.	1937	140.00	70.00
338	L20	Mount Everest	1925	96.00	48.00
725	L32	Myths & Legends (Tom Thumb Cigars)	1981	28.00	—
238	25	Napoleon	1915	54.00	24.00
	25	Napoleon (Black back) A.A.	Unissued	—	—
5402	D24	Napoleonic Uniforms (Doncella Cigars)	1979	6.50	—
83	D1	Napoleonic Uniforms (Completion Offer) (Doncella Cigars)	1979	2.25	—
1	50	National Flags & Arms	1936	22.00	11.00
	50	National Flags & Arms (Irish Issue) A.A.	1936	70.00	35.00
	50	National Flags & Arms (Overseas, no I.T.C.) A.A.	1936	56.00	28.00
252	50	Natural History	1924	26.00	13.00
1134	X12	Natural History 1st Series (as set 252)	1924	26.00	13.00
1135	X12	Natural History 2nd Series (as set 252)	1924	26.00	13.00
307	50	Nature Series	1908	150.00	70.00
45	X10	Nature Series (Animals) (as set 307)	1913	80.00	40.00
	X10	Nature Series (Birds) (as set 307)	1908	180.00	90.00
1377	50	Old England's Defenders	1898	1800.00	900.00
266	L25	Old Hunting Prints	1938	150.00	75.00
	L25	Old Hunting Prints (Overseas, no I.T.C.) A.A.	1938	160.00	80.00
328	L25	Old Naval Prints	1936	120.00	60.00
	L25	Old Naval Prints (Overseas, no I.T.C.) A.A.	1936	140.00	70.00
1137	X25	Old Sporting Prints	1924	110.00	55.00

Ref. No.	No. in Set	Name of Set	Date	COMPLETE SETS Grade 1	Grade 2
		JOHN PLAYER & SONS (Cont'd)			
	D8	Panama Puzzles (Panama)	1974	45.00	30.00
340	L25	Picturesque Bridges	1929	120.00	60.00
323	L25	Picturesque Cottages	1929	130.00	65.00
329	L25	Picturesque London	1931	160.00	80.00
	48	Pictures of the East (Overseas, no I.T.C.)	1931	75.00	50.00
	25	Picturesque People of the Empire (Overseas, no I.T.C.)	1938	70.00	45.00
216	25	Players — Past & Present	1916	36.00	16.00
	D6	Play Ladbroke Spot Ball (Panama)	1975	36.00	24.00
	D6	Play Panama Spot Six (Panama)	1977	36.00	24.00
	B53	Playing Cards (Overseas)	1929	104.00	52.00
183	25	Polar Exploration 1st Series	1911	74.00	32.00
303	25	Polar Exploration 2nd Series	1916	74.00	32.00
325	L25	Portals of the Past	1930	120.00	60.00
100	50	Poultry	1931	100.00	50.00
369	50	Poultry (Transfers) A.A.	1931	16.00	10.00
1367	25	Products of the World	1909	24.00	12.00
137	50	Products of the World	1928	20.00	10.00
	50	Products of the World (Black back)	Unissued	—	—
	50	Pugilists in Action (Drumhead)	1928	180.00	90.00
3141	25	Racehorses	1926	220.00	110.00
185	40	Racing Caricatures	1925	60.00	30.00
320	L25	Racing Yachts	1938	160.00	80.00
	L25	Racing Yachts (Overseas, no I.T.C.) A.A.	1938	170.00	85.00
193	50	RAF Badges (with motto)	·1937	50.00	25.00
56	50	RAF Badges (without motto) A.A.	1937	50.00	25.00
	50	RAF Badges (Overseas, no I.T.C.) A.A.	1937	70.00	35.00
1577	50	Railway Working (Overseas)	1926	150.00	75.00
311	50	Regimental Colours & Cap Badges (Regulars)	1907	90.00	45.00
312	50	Regimental Colours & Cap Badges (Territorials Blue)	1910	90.00	45.00
1572	50	Regimental Colours & Cap Badges (Territorials Brown) A.A.	1910	90.00	45.00
505	50	Regimental Standards & Cap Badges	1930	64.00	32.00
132	50	Regimental Uniforms 1st Series (Blue)	1912	170.00	80.00
306	50	Regimental Uniforms 1st Series (Brown) A.A.	1914	180.00	85.00
2679	X10	Regimental Uniforms (also issued as Allied Cavalry)	1914	144.00	72.00

Ref. No.	No. in Set	Name of Set	Date	COMPLETE SETS Grade 1	Grade 2

JOHN PLAYER & SONS (Cont'd)

Ref. No.	No. in Set	Name of Set	Date	Grade 1	Grade 2
232	50	Regimental Uniforms 2nd Series	1914	150.00	70.00
134	50	Riders of the World	1905	160.00	75.00
	S30	Rulers & Views (F)	1902	—	—
1575	50	Screen Celebrities (Irish Issue)	1939	110.00	55.00
55	50	Sea Fishes	1935	24.00	12.00
	50	Sea Fishes (Irish Issue) A.A.	1935	70.00	35.00
	50	Sea Fishes (Overseas) A.A.	1935	64.00	32.00
304	25	Shakespearean Series	1916	35.00	15.00
1138	L20	Ships Models	1926	110.00	55.00
4181	50	Shipping	Unissued	90.00	60.00
305	25	Ships' Figureheads	1912	54.00	24.00
330	L25	Ships' Figureheads	1931	72.00	36.00
	50	Ships' Flags & Cap Badges (Overseas)	1930	120.00	60.00
	50	Signalling Series (Overseas)	1926	120.00	60.00
	L8	Snap Cards	1930	96.00	56.00
23	50	Speedway Riders	1937	110.00	55.00
	150	Stereoscopic Series	1904	—	—
268	50	Straight Line Caricatures	1926	44.00	22.00
191	25	Struggle for Existance	1923	8.25	5.25
24	50	Tennis	1936	50.00	25.00
	116	The Corsair Game (Irish Issue)	1965	—	—
3908	D24	The Golden Age of Flying (Doncella Cigars)	1977	5.50	—
	D1	The Golden Age of Flying (Completion offer) (Doncella Cigars)	1977	1.50	—
1804	D24	The Golden Age of Motoring (Doncella Cigars)	1975	7.00	—
	D24	The Golden Age of Motoring (Completion offer) (Doncella Cigars) A.A.	1975	60.00	—
2581	D24	The Golden Age of Sail (Doncella Cigars)	1978	5.50	—
84	D1	The Golden Age of Sail (Completion offer) (Doncella Cigars)	1978	2.00	—
3364	D24	The Golden Age of Steam (Doncella Cigars)	1976	6.50	—
	D1	The Golden Age of Steam (Completion offer) (Doncella Cigars)	1976	2.00	—
1604	D30	The Living Ocean (Doncella)	1985	6.50	—
1605	D30	The Living Ocean (Grandee)	1985	8.00	—
321	L25	The Nation's Shrines	1929	92.00	46.00
5244	P6	The Royal Family (F)	1902	450.00	225.00

A SELECTION FROM PLAYER'S

SET No: 134

SET No: 320

SET No: 137

SET No: 505

SET No: 305

SET No: 268

SET No: 328

Ref. No.	No. in Set	Name of Set	Date	COMPLETE SETS Grade 1	Grade 2
		JOHN PLAYER & SONS (Cont'd)			
596	L1	The Royal Family	1937	5.00	2.50
	50	The Royal Family at Home & Abroad (Overseas) (F)	1927	75.00	50.00
445	25	Those Pearls of Heaven	1914	28.00	14.00
	X4	Tom Thumb Record Breakers	1976	—	—
5484	D25	Top Dogs (Grandee Cigars)	1976	17.00	—
	66	Transvaal Series	1902	600.00	300.00
333	L25	Treasures of Britain	1931	90.00	45.00
2260	25	Treasures of Ireland	1930	88.00	44.00
646	L25	Types of Horses	1939	130.00	65.00
	L25	Types of Horses (Overseas) A.A.	1939	150.00	75.00
7	50	Uniforms of the Territorial Army	1939	60.00	30.00
1036	50	Useful Plants & Fruits	1904	150.00	75.00
233	25	Victoria Cross	1914	64.00	32.00
411	90	War Decorations & Medals	1927	92.00	46.00
1520	25	Whaling (Overseas)	1930	100.00	50.00
247	50	Wild Animals' Heads	1931	40.00	20.00
1371	50	Wild Animals' Heads (Transfers) A.A.	1931	16.00	10.00
1140	L25	Wild Animals 1st Series (as set 247)	1927	80.00	40.00
1141	L25	Wild Animals 2nd Series (as set 247)	1932	80.00	40.00
1399	50	Wild Animals of the World (no Ltd.)	1901	240.00	120.00
827	50	Wild Animals of the World (Wide card) (with Ltd.) A.A.	1901	240.00	120.00
	45	Wild Animals of the World (Narrow card) (no Ltd.) A.A.	1901	360.00	180.00
	45	Wild Animals of the World (Narrow card) (with Ltd.) A.A.	1901	360.00	180.00
227	50	Wild Birds	1932	28.00	14.00
345	50	Wild Birds (Transfers) A.A.	1932	16.00	10.00
1307	L25	Wild Birds A.A.	1934	100.00	50.00
804	L25	Wild Fowl	1937	120.00	60.00
1632	L32	Wonders of the Ancient World (Tom Thumb)	1984	8.50	—
1368	50	Wonders of the Deep	1904	150.00	75.00
	50	Wonders of the Deep (Black back) A.A.	Unissued	—	—
1633	L30	Wonders of the Modern World (Tom Thumb)	1985	9.00	—
251	25	Wonders of the World (Blue back)	1916	32.00	16.00
2257	25	Wonders of the World (Grey back) A.A.	1926	40.00	24.00
	25	Wonders of the World (Black back) A.A.	Unissued	—	—

A SELECTION FROM PLAYER'S

SET No: 411

SET No: 1142

SET No: 251

SET No: 308

SET No: 80

SET No: 247

SET No: 7

Ref. No.	No. in Set	Name of Set	Date	COMPLETE SETS Grade 1	Grade 2
		JOHN PLAYER & SONS (Cont'd)			
1729	X10	Wooden Walls	1909	100.00	50.00
	D6	World of Gardening	1976	—	—
308	25	Wrestling & Ju-Jitsu (Blue back)	1911	40.00	20.00
2792	25	Wrestling & Ju-Jitsu (Grey back) A.A.	1925	48.00	28.00
1375	26	Your Initials (Transfers)	1932	12.00	8.00
1142	L25	Zoo Babies	1938	20.00	10.00
	L25	Zoo Babies (Overseas) A.A.	1937	72.00	36.00
		PRITCHARD & BURTON			
	50	Actors & Actresses (FROGA)	1900	1600.00	800.00
	15	Beauties (PAC)	1900	1600.00	800.00
	20	Boer War Cartoons	1900	3100.00	1550.00
1669	30	Flags & Flags with Soldiers (Flagstaff draped)	1901	780.00	390.00
	15	Flags & Flags with Soldiers (Flagstaff undraped) A.A.	1901	540.00	270.00
	25	Holiday Resorts & Views	1902	800.00	400.00
	40	Home & Colonial Regiments	1901	3600.00	1800.00
	25	Royalty Series	1902	980.00	490.00
	25	South African Series	1901	800.00	400.00
	25	Star Girls	1900	5500.00	2750.00
		ROTHMANS LTD.			
2068	40	Beauties of the Cinema	1939	90.00	45.00
2069	L24	Beauties of the Cinema (Circular)	1939	150.00	75.00
2070	24	Cinema Stars (F)	1933	35.00	20.00
2072	L25	Cinema Stars (F)	1933	38.00	22.00
140	P30	Country Living Cards	1974	15.00	10.00
	P6	Diamond Jubilee Folders	1950	—	—
2198	36	Landmarks in Empire History	1936	80.00	40.00
142	50	Modern Inventions	1935	80.00	40.00
3774	L54	New Zealand (F)	1933	48.00	32.00
838	24	Prominent Screen Favourites	1934	38.00	22.00
2071	50	Punch Jokes (F)	1935	40.00	20.00
	D5	Rare Banknotes (Folders)	1970	18.00	10.00

A SELECTION OF ROYALTY SETS

SET 131

SET 182

GOD. PHIL SET 207

SET 1115

OGDEN SET 2251

SET 2137

CAR SET 3733

Ref. No.	No. in Set	Name of Set	Date	Grade 1	Grade 2
		COMPLETE SETS			
		WM. RUDDELL LTD.			
50	25	Grand Opera Series	1924	325.00	175.00
	?1	Miniature Couplet Cards	1925	—	—
4108	25	Rod & Gun	1924	250.00	135.00
1992	50	Songs That Will Live For Ever	1924	255.00	145.00
		SALMON & GLUCKSTEIN LTD.			
	X1	Advertisement Card (Snake Charmer)	1898	760.00	380.00
	15	Billiard Terms	1906	1360.00	680.00
	12	British Queens	1897	950.00	475.00
826	X30	Castles, Abbeys & Houses (Brown back)	1906	900.00	450.00
	X30	Castles, Abbeys & Houses (Red back) A.A.	1906	1250.00	625.00
	32	Characters from Dickens	1904	1450.00	725.00
2286	25	Coronation Series	1911	400.00	200.00
	L25	Famous Pictures (Brown)	1912	440.00	220.00
	L25	Famous Pictures (Green, Different)	1912	350.00	175.00
3734	6	Her Most Gracious Majesty Queen Victoria	1897	560.00	280.00
	40	Heroes of the Transvaal War	1901	1250.00	625.00
2424	25	Magical Series	1923	180.00	90.00
	30	Music Hall Celebrities	1903	2500.00	1250.00
	?26	Occupations and Comics	1898	—	—
	20	Owners & Jockeys Series	1906	1950.00	975.00
	L50	Pottery Types (Silk Nd. back only)	1916	340.00	170.00
	L50	Pottery Types (Silk Nd. front & back) A.A.	1916	340.00	170.00
	6	Pretty Girl Series (RASH)	1900	740.00	370.00
4019	22	Shakespearian Series	1902	1000.00	500.00
	25	Star Girls (Brown back)	1899	5600.00	2800.00
	25	Star Girls (Red back) A.A.	1899	5600.00	2800.00
	50	The Great White City	1909	1020.00	510.00
	48	The Post in Various Countries	1901	2200.00	1100.00
316	25	Traditions of the Army & Navy	1917	450.00	225.00
3139	25	Wireless Explained	1923	200.00	100.00

Ref. No.	No. in Set	Name of Set	Date	Grade 1	Grade 2
		W. SANDORIDES & CO. LTD.			
	25	Aquarium Studies from the London Zoo	1925	90.00	60.00
3856	L25	Aqarium Studies from the London Zoo A.A.	1925	90.00	60.00
1285	25	Cinema Celebrities	1924	115.00	65.00
	P25	Cinema Celebrities A.A.	1924	180.00	100.00
	25	Cinema Stars (Export firm's name)	1924	260.00	140.00
	25	Cinema Stars (Export Lucana Cigs.) A.A.	1924	260.00	140.00
	25	Cinema Stars (Export Big Gun Cigs.) A.A.	1924	290.00	170.00
	P25	Cinema Stars (Export Big Gun Cigs.) A.A.	1924	110.00	70.00
	P25	Cinema Stars (Export Lucana 66 Cigs.) A.A.	1924	285.00	165.00
5537	50	Famous Racecourses	1926	160.00	100.00
3857	L50	Famous Racecourses A.A.	1926	235.00	135.00
3273	50	Famous Racehorses	1923	170.00	90.00
	25	Sports & Pastimes	1924	475.00	275.00

SANSOM'S CIGAR STORES

?13		London Views	1910	4200.00	2100.00

Ref. No.	No. in Set	Name of Set	Date	COMPLETE SETS Grade 1	Grade 2
		NICHOLAS SARONY & CO.			
443	25	A Day on the Airway	1928	44.00	22.00
2466	L25	A Day on the Airway	1928	60.00	30.00
1517	50	Around the Mediterranean	1926	60.00	35.00
1736	L50	Around the Mediterranean	1926	60.00	35.00
	?M1	Boer War Scenes	1901	400.00	200.00
1816	25	Celebrities & Their Authographs (1-25)	1923	24.00	12.00
1192	L25	Celebrities & Their Autographs (1-25)	1923	24.00	12.00
1818	25	Celebrities & Their Autographs (26-50)	1924	24.00	12.00
1193	L25	Celebrities & Their Autographs (26-50)	1924	24.00	12.00
1819	25	Celebrities & Their Autographs (51-75)	1924	24.00	12.00
1311	L25	Celebrities & Their Autographs (51-75)	1924	24.00	12.00
1820	25	Celebrities & Their Autographs (76-100)	1925	24.00	12.00
1194	L25	Celebrities & Their Autographs (76−100)	1925	24.00	12.00
2050	50	Cinema Stars	1933	75.00	45.00
	P38	Cinema Stars, 1st Series (F)	1929	660.00	330.00
5493	P42	Cinema Stars, 2nd Series (F)	1929	400.00	200.00
5521	P50	Cinema Stars, 3rd Series (F)	1930	450.00	225.00
5522	P42	Cinema Stars, 4th Series (F)	1930	400.00	200.00
5494	P25	Cinema Stars, 5th Series (F)	1930	220.00	110.00
2049	25	Cinema Studies	1929	44.00	22.00
1516	54	Life at Whipsnade Zoo (F)	1934	36.00	24.00
529	25	Links with the Past (first 25 subjects No. 1-25)	1925	12.00	6.00
1195	L25	Links with the Past (first 25 subjects No. 1-25) A.A.	1925	12.00	6.00
2269	25	Links with the Past (second 25 subjects No. 26-50)	1925	12.00	6.00
1203	L25	Links with the Past (second 25 subjects No. 26-50) A.A.	1925	12.00	6.00
723	L26	Links with the Past (Advertisement back) A.A.	1925	50.00	25.00
729	25	Links with the Past (Aust. Issue) A.A.	1925	22.00	11.00
730	L25	Links with the Past (Aust. Issue) A.A.	1925	22.00	11.00
731	25	Links with the Past (N.Z. Issue) A.A.	1925	22.00	11.00
733	L25	Links with the Past (N.Z. Issue) A.A.	1925	20.00	10.00
2270	25	Museum Series	1927	14.00	7.00
1196	L25	Museum Series	1927	12.00	6.00
734	L25	Museum Series (Advertisement back) A.A.	1927	24.00	12.00
735	L25	Museum Series (Aust. Issue) A.A.	1927	20.00	10.00
736	25	Museum Series (N.Z. Issue) A.A.	1927	20.00	10.00

A SELECTION FROM SARONY ETC.

SET No: 2044

SET No: 3273

SET No: 1093

SET No: 1972

SET No: 1094

SET No: 2051

SET No: 1216

Ref. No.	No. in Set	Name of Set	Date	Grade 1	Grade 2
		NICHOLAS SARONY & CO. (Cont'd)			
737	L25	Museum Series (N.Z. Issue) A.A.	1927	20.00	10.00
1215	36	National Types of Beauty (F)	1928	22.00	11.00
1972	M36	National Types of Beauty (F)	1928	20.00	12.00
1748	15	Origin of Games	1923	72.00	36.00
3457	L15	Origin of Games	1923	80.00	40.00
2052	50	Saronicks	1929	20.00	10.00
2051	M50	Saronicks	1929	20.00	10.00
97	50	Ships of All Ages	1929	35.00	20.00
2044	M50	Ships of All Ages	1929	35.00	20.00
1216	25	Tennis Strokes	1923	100.00	50.00

SCOTTISH C.W.S.

Ref. No.	No. in Set	Name of Set	Date	Grade 1	Grade 2
624	25	Burns (printed back)	1924	48.00	24.00
	25	Burns (plain back) A.A.	1924	110.00	55.00
	20	Dogs	1925	320.00	180.00
2280	25	Dwellings of All Nations (printed back)	1924	90.00	45.00
	25	Dwellings of All Nations (plain back) A.A.	1924	250.00	125.00
5455	L25	Famous Pictures	1924	250.00	130.00
107	L25	Famous Pictures — Glasgow Galleries (Adhesive)	1927	52.00	26.00
108	L25	Famous Pictures — Glasgow Galleries (Non-adhesive)	1927	90.00	45.00
380	L25	Famous Pictures — London Galleries (Adhesive)	1927	56.00	28.00
1837	L25	Famous Pictures — London Galleries (Non-adhesive)	1927	90.00	45.00
625	50	Feathered Favourites (Adhesive)	1926	105.00	55.00
109	50	Feathered Favourites (Non-adhesive)	1926	140.00	80.00
3488	25	Racial Types	1925	350.00	175.00
110	50	Triumphs of Engineering (Brown border)	1926	180.00	90.00
	50	Triumphs of Engineering (White border) A.A.	1926	180.00	90.00
111	50	Wireless	1924	225.00	115.00

Ref. No.	No. in Set	Name of Set	Date	COMPLETE SETS Grade 1	Grade 2
		JOHN SINCLAIR LTD.			
	B?62	Actresses (Black & White)	1901	—	—
	48	Birds (Descriptive back) (F)	1924	160.00	80.00
	48	Birds (Specimen cigarette card) (F) A.A.	1924	425.00	225.00
	L50	Birds (Descriptive back) (F) A.A.	1924	360.00	200.00
2754	50	British Sea Dogs	1926	350.00	175.00
1093	54	Champion Dogs 1st Series (F)	1938	44.00	22.00
1202	L52	Champion Dogs 1st Series (F)	1938	52.00	26.00
1094	54	Champion Dogs 2nd Series (F)	1939	220.00	110.00
58	L52	Champion Dogs 2nd Series (F)	1939	250.00	125.00
842	50	English & Scottish Football Stars (F)	1935	90.00	45.00
1095	54	Film Stars (Series of 54 Real Photos) (F)	1934	130.00	70.00
1096	54	Film Stars (Series of Real Photos) (F)	1937	110.00	60.00
2045	54	Film Stars (55-108) (F)	1937	110.00	60.00
	M50	Flags, 4th Series (Silk)	1914	480.00	240.00
	M50	Flags, 5th Series (Silk)	1914	480.00	240.00
L	& X50	Flags, 6th Series (Silk)	1914	600.00	300.00
	S10	Flags, 7th Series (Silk)	1914	800.00	400.00
	96	Flowers & Plants (Descriptive back) (F)	1924	200.00	130.00
	96	Flowers & Plants (Specimen cigarette card) (F) A.A.	1924	460.00	300.00
	L96	Flowers & Plants (Descriptive back) (F) A.A.	1924	340.00	220.00
	50	Football Favourites (No. 51-100) (F)	1908	6000.00	3000.00
	4	North Country Celebrities	1905	420.00	210.00
	?80	Northern Gems (F)	1902	—	—
	50	Picture Puzzles & Riddle Series	1916	1900.00	950.00
1405	54	Radio Favourites (F)	1935	140.00	70.00
	K35	Rubicon Cards (Miniature P/C)	1935	330.00	210.00
	50	Trick Series	1916	1900.00	950.00
784	50	Well Known Footballers (N.E. Counties)	1938	84.00	42.00
2046	50	Well Known Footballers (Scottish)	1938	80.00	40.00
874	50	World's Coinage	1915	1550.00	775.00
		ROBERT SINCLAIR TOBACCO CO. LTD.			
	X?4	Battleships & Crests (Silk)	1916	370.00	185.00
	10	Billiards 1st Set (No. 1-10)	1928	110.00	55.00
4182	15	Billiards 2nd Set (No. 11-25)	1928	170.00	85.00
	3	Billiards 3rd Set (Nos. 26/28 only issued)	1928	50.00	25.00
	28	Dominoes	1903	—	—
	?M8	Flags (Silk)	1916	400.00	200.00

Ref. No.	No. in Set	Name of Set	Date	COMPLETE SETS Grade 1	Grade 2

ROBERET SINCLAIR TOBACCO CO. LTD. (Cont'd)

Ref. No.	No. in Set	Name of Set	Date	Grade 1	Grade 2
	?5	Footballers	1900	—	—
	P?6	Great War Area (Silk)	1916	480.00	240.00
	M10	Great War Heroes (Silk)	1916	700.00	350.00
	12	Policemen of the World	1899	3100.00	1550.00
	X?1	Red Cross Nurse (Silk)	1916	100.00	50.00
	M?5	Regimental Badges (Silk)	1916	260.00	130.00
	12	The Smiler Series	1924	120.00	60.00
	L12	The Smiler Series	1924	200.00	100.00

J. SINFIELD

Ref. No.	No. in Set	Name of Set	Date	Grade 1	Grade 2
	24	Beauties (HUMPS)	1898	—	—

SINGLETON & COLE LTD.

Ref. No.	No. in Set	Name of Set	Date	Grade 1	Grade 2
	50	Atlantic Liners	1910	1600.00	800.00
87	25	Bonzo Series	1928	220.00	110.00
3614	50	Celebrities (Actresses & Boer War)	1901	1520.00	760.00
	110	Crest & Badges of the British Army (Silk)	1916	850.00	425.00
	35	Famous Boxers (Numbered)	1930	530.00	265.00
	35	Famous Boxers (Unnumbered) A.A.	1930	—	—
	25	Famous Film Stars	1930	360.00	180.00
689	35	Famous Officers (Hero Series)	1915	—	—
	50	Footballers	1905	6000.00	3000.00
	40	Kings & Queens	1902	1200.00	600.00
	B12	Manikin Cards (with Horoscope panel)	1915	1500.00	750.00
	25	Maxims of Success	1907	1120.00	560.00
	8	Orient Royal Mail Line (Firm's name back)	1905	620.00	310.00
	8	Orient Royal Mail Line (Orient-Pacific Line back) A.A.	1905	750.00	375.00
	25	The Wallace-Jones Keep Fit System	1911	880.00	440.00

THE SINSOCK & CO. (KOREA)

Ref. No.	No. in Set	Name of Set	Date	Grade 1	Grade 2
	?20	Korean Girls	1902	950.00	475.00

A SELECTION FROM JOHN SINCLAIR ETC.

SET No: 784

SET No: 842

SET No: 2046

SET No: 1095

SET No: 1096

SET No: 2045

SET No: 1405

SET No: 689

SET No: 87

Ref. No.	No. in Set	Name of Set	Date	COMPLETE SETS Grade 1	Grade 2
		F. & J. SMITH			
	25	Advertisement Cards	1899	—	—
692	50	A Tour Round the World (Advertisement back)	1904	2200.00	1100.00
	50	A Tour Round the World (Post-Card back)	1905	3800.00	1900.00
	50	A Tour Round the World (Descriptive)	1906	680.00	340.00
1630	50	Battlefields of Great Britain	1913	1080.00	540.00
	25	Boer War Series (Black & White)	1900	2500.00	1250.00
3494	50	Boer War Series (Coloured)	1900	2300.00	1150.00
	50	Champions of Sport (Blue back)	1903	5000.00	2500.00
	50	Champions of Sport (Red back)	1903	4600.00	2300.00
1763	25	Cinema Stars	1920	280.00	140.00
1839	50	Cricketers, 1st Series	1912	1200.00	600.00
5569	20	Cricketers, 2nd Series (Nd. 51-70)	1912	1200.00	600.00
1688	50	Derby Winners	1913	1100.00	550.00
885	50	Famous Explorers	1911	960.00	480.00
	50	Football Club Records (1913-1917)	1918	920.00	460.00
	50	Football Club Records (1921-1922)	1922	820.00	410.00
	120	Footballers (Brown back)	1905	5000.00	2500.00
	100	Footballers (Blue back)	1909	1650.00	825.00
	150	Footballers (Yellow Frame Line)	1913	2200.00	1100.00
2425	50	Fowls, Pigeons & Dogs	1908	700.00	350.00
	25	Holiday Resorts	1925	320.00	160.00
	50	Medals (Imperial Tobacco Co. Ltd. back Nd.)	1903	—	—
1555	50	Medals (Imperial Tobacco Co. back Nd.)	1906	800.00	400.00
	50	Medals (Smith back Nd.)	1902	650.00	325.00
944	20	Medals (Unnumbered)	1905	450.00	225.00
	50	Nations of the World	1923	520.00	260.00
691	50	Naval Dress & Badges (Descriptive back)	1911	760.00	380.00
	50	Naval Dress & Badges (Non-descriptive back) A.A.	1914	760.00	380.00
3491	50	Phil May Sketches (Brown back)	1924	450.00	225.00
	50	Phil May Sketches (Grey back)	1908	700.00	350.00
	25	Prominent Rugby Players	1924	450.00	225.00
	40	Races of Mankind (with series title)	1900	3400.00	1700.00
	40	Races of Mankind (without series title) A.A.	1900	4400.00	2200.00
2318	25	Shadowgraphs	1915	190.00	95.00
	25	War Incidents 1st Series	1914	200.00	100.00
690	25	War Incidents 2nd Series	1915	200.00	100.00

A SELECTION OF AVIATION SETS

CARRERAS SET 1223

SET 448

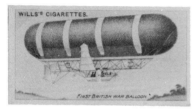

SET 166

HILL SET 2191

SET 419

ARDATH SET 1879

SET 1102

SET 47

COMPLETE SETS

Ref. No.	No. in Set	Name of Set	Date	Grade 1	Grade 2
		TADDY & CO.			
	?72	Actresses, Collotype (Plain backs)	1897	12400.00	6200.00
	25	Actresses with Flowers	1899	3700.00	1850.00
	37	Admirals & Generals — The War	1915	1450.00	725.00
	25	Admirals & Generals — The War (South African Issue)	1915	1800.00	900.00
	1	Advertisement Card (Imperial Tobacco)	1900	—	—
1657	25	Autographs	1912	750.00	375.00
1612	20	Boer Leaders	1901	650.00	325.00
1387	50	British Medals & Decorations Series 2	1909	860.00	430.00
1386	50	British Medals & Ribbons	1907	860.00	430.00
	20	Clowns & Circus Artistes (Plain backs)	—	25000.00	12500.00
1975	30	Coronation Series	1902	1100.00	550.00
	238	County Cricketers	1907	16400.00	8200.00
693	50	Dogs	1901	2000.00	1000.00
	5	English Royalty	1897	4800.00	2400.00
3684	25	Famous Actors — Famous Actresses	1903	800.00	400.00
	50	Famous Horses & Cattle	1908	8500.00	4250.00
1566	25	Famous Jockeys (With Frame)	1911	1100.00	550.00
	25	Famous Jockeys (Without Frame)	1911	1200.00	600.00
	50	Footballers (New Zealand)	1901	5800.00	2900.00
1288	25	Heraldry Series	1911	650.00	325.00
2337	25	Honours & Ribbons	1906	780.00	390.00
1826	10	Klondyke Series	1900	1150.00	575.00
	60	Leading Members of the Legislative Assembly (South Africa)	1901	—	—
	25	Natives of the World	1899	2400.00	1200.00
3121	25	Orders of Chivalry	1911	850.00	425.00
1801	25	Orders of Chivalry 2nd Series	1912	1600.00	800.00
	595	Prominent Footballers (Grapnel or Imperial Back without Footnote)	1907	8600.00	4300.00
	400	Prominent Footballers (Grapnel or Imperial Back with Footnote)	1909	6200.00	3100.00
	?347	Prominent Footballers (London Mixture Back)	1913	—	—
	20	Royalty, Actresses & Soldiers	1898	7200.00	3600.00
3214	25	Royalty Series	1903	950.00	475.00
833	25	Russo Japanese War (Nd. 1-25)	1904	650.00	325.00
834	25	Russo Japanese War (Nd. 26-50)	1904	900.00	450.00
	16	South African Cricket Team, 1907	1907	1550.00	775.00
	26	South African Football Team, 1906-7	1907	1020.00	510.00
1656	25	Sports & Pastimes	1912	800.00	400.00
1655	25	Territorial Regiments	1908	900.00	450.00

A SELECTION OF SETS ON DOGS

SET 1148

SET 139

SET 2059

SET 125

GODFREY PHILLIPS
SET 1190

SET 1149

SET 287

Ref. No.	No. in Set	Name of Set	Date	**COMPLETE SETS** Grade 1	Grade 2
		TADDY & CO. (Cont'd)			
	25	Thames Series	1903	1600.00	800.00
837	20	Victoria Cross Heroes (Nd. 1-20)	1901	1850.00	925.00
694	20	Victoria Cross Heroes (Nd. 21-40)	1901	1650.00	825.00
1420	20	VC Heroes — Boer War (Nd. 41—60)	1902	600.00	300.00
695	20	VC Heroes — Boer War (Nd. 61-80)	1902	600.00	300.00
712	20	VC Heroes — Boer War (Nd. 81-100)	1902	700.00	350.00
	25	Victoria Cross Heroes (Nd. 101-125)	1904	2500.00	1250.00
5591	2	Wrestlers (F)	1909	1000.00	500.00

TEOFANI & CO. LTD.

Ref. No.	No. in Set	Name of Set	Date	Grade 1	Grade 2
	25	Aquarium Studies from the London Zoo	1925	315.00	210.00
	50	Cinema Celebrities (Broadway Novelties)	1926	280.00	160.00
	50	Cinema Celebrities (Well-known cigs.) A.A.	1926	250.00	130.00
	25	Cinema Stars (Anonymous) A.A.	1926	140.00	80.00
	P25	Cinema Stars (Anonymous) A.A.	1926	200.00	120.00
	25	Cinema Stars (Blue Band Cigarettes) A.A.	1926	315.00	165.00
	25	Cinema Stars (Three Star Cigarettes) A.A.	1926	315.00	165.00
883	25	Cinema Stars (Three Star Magnums) A.A.	1926	315.00	165.00
	P25	Cinema Stars (Three Star Magnums) A.A.	1926	235.00	125.00
	25	Famous Boxers (Export)	1926	300.00	150.00
2860	32	Famous British Ships & Officers (Export) (F)	1934	115.00	65.00
	50	Famous Racecourses	1926	—	—
	50	Famous Racehorses	1927	650.00	410.00
2195	12	Film Actors & Actresses (Plain Back Export)	1937	10.00	6.00
	20	Great Inventors (Export)	1924	125.00	75.00
888	20	Head dresses of Various Nations (Plain Back Export)	1926	390.00	190.00
2096	12	London Views (Plain Back) (Export)	1936	7.00	4.00

A SELECTION FROM TADDY & CO.

SET No: 1566

SET No: 1386

SET No: 693

SET No: 3121

SET No: 1288

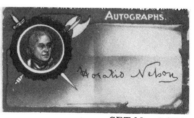

SET No: 1657

SET No: 1387

SET No: 3241

SET No: 1975

Ref. No.	No. in Set	Name of Set	Date	COMPLETE SETS Grade 1	Grade 2
		TEOFANI & CO. LTD.(Cont'd)			
2097	48	Modern Movie Stars & Cinema Celebrities (Export)	1934	46.00	26.00
	50	Natives in Costume (Plain back)	1926	950.00	550.00
2142	24	Past & Present (A — The Army Nd. 1-24)	1938	40.00	25.00
1441	24	Past & Present (B — Weapons of War Nd. 25–48)	1938	20.00	12.50
	52	Past & Present (C — Transport Nd. 49-100)	1939	—	—
	50	Public Schools & Colleges (Export)	1924	250.00	150.00
1402	50	Ships & Their Flags (Export)	1925	250.00	125.00
	25	Sports & Pastimes (Plain back) (Export)	1924	160.00	80.00
	25	Sports & Pastimes (Printed back) A.A.	1924	520.00	260.00
	22	Teofani Gems (Plain back) (Export)	1925	85.00	45.00
	28	Teofani Gems (Plain back) (Export)	1925	40.00	20.00
	36	Teofani Gems (Plain back) (Export)	1925	144.00	72.00
	50	Teofani's Icelandic Employees (F)	1930	375.00	225.00
696	48	Transport Then & Now (Export)	1939	28.00	16.00
	50	Views of London (Export)	1925	200.00	100.00
	36	Views of the British Empire (Export) (F)	1927	65.00	35.00
	24	Well Known Racehorses (Export)	1923	220.00	120.00
	50	Worlds Smokers (Plain back)	1926	1050.00	525.00
	50	Zoological Studies (Export)	1924	250.00	150.00
		TETLEY & SONS LTD.			
	1	"The Allies" (Grouped Flags)	1916	420.00	210.00
	50	War Portraits	1916	5600.00	2800.00
697	25	World's Coinage (Oracle Back)	1913	2300.00	1150.00
		UNITED KINGDOM TOBACCO CO. LTD.			
3688	50	Aircraft (Greys Cigarettes)	1933	100.00	50.00
114	P48	Beautiful Britain (Greys Cigarettes)	1929	54.00	36.00
115	P48	Beautiful Britain 2nd Series (Greys Cigarettes)	1929	54.00	36.00
2143	25	British Orders of Chivalry & Valour (Greys Cigarettes)	1936	44.00	24.00
533	24	Chinese Scenes	1933	14.00	8.00
2162	32	Cinema Stars	1933	72.00	36.00

A SELECTION FROM TADDY & CO. & TEOFANI

SET No: 694

SET No: 1420

SET No: 695

SET No: 2142

SET No: 712

SET No: 2097

SET No: 1441

SET No: 1402

				COMPLETE SETS	
Ref. No.	No. in Set	Name of Set	Date	Grade 1	Grade 2

UNITED KINGDOM TOBACCO CO. LTD.(Cont'd)

Ref. No.	No. in Set	Name of Set	Date	Grade 1	Grade 2
2421	50	Cinema Stars (Anonymous back)	1934	80.00	50.00
	50	Cinema Stars (Firm's name) A.A.	1934	80.00	50.00
11	36	Officers Full Dress	1936	80.00	40.00
510	36	Soldiers of the King (Greys Cigarettes)	1937	66.00	36.00

UNITED SERVICES MFG. CO.

Ref. No.	No. in Set	Name of Set	Date	Grade 1	Grade 2
2993	50	Ancient Warriors	1938	95.00	55.00
2994	25	Ancient Warriors (Reprint First 25 numbers of above set)	1957	125.00	75.00
2131	50	Bathing Belles	1939	40.00	24.00
	100	Interesting Personalities	1935	280.00	170.00
3763	50	Popular Footballers	1936	260.00	130.00
3762	50	Popular Screen Stars	1937	250.00	125.00

W. D. & H. O. WILLS LTD.

Ref. No.	No. in Set	Name of Set	Date	Grade 1	Grade 2
3129	52	Actresses (P/C Inset) Brown Back	1898	1400.00	700.00
	52	Actresses (P/C Inset) Grey Back	1897	1500.00	750.00
	52	Actresses (Without P/C Inset) Grey Back	1897	1600.00	800.00
	25	Actresses, Collotype	1895	3300.00	1650.00
	50	Actresses & Celebrities Collotype	1895	8400.00	4200.00
	25	Advertisement Cards	1899	16200.00	8100.00
116	1	Advertisement Card (Three Castles)	1965	2.00	1.00
117	L1	Advertisement Card (Wants List)	1935	1.20	0.60
66	50	Air Raid Precautions	1938	28.00	14.00
	40	Air Raid Precautions (Eire — non-adhesive) A.A.	1938	64.00	32.00
317	50	Allied Army Leaders	1917	140.00	65.00
211	50	Alpine Flowers	1913	74.00	32.00
118	49	And When Did You Last See Your Father (Sect.)	1932	72.00	36.00
	50	Animals & Birds in Fancy Costume	1896	4400.00	2200.00
1210	48	Animalloys (Sect.)	1934	24.00	12.00
1301	L25	Animals & Their Furs	1929	85.00	45.00
231	50	Arms of Companies	1913	62.00	28.00
165	50	Arms of Foreign Cities	1912	70.00	30.00
350	L42	Arms of Oxford & Cambridge Colleges	1922	90.00	45.00
2202	L25	Arms of Public Schools 1st Series	1933	70.00	35.00
2197	L25	Arms of Public Schools 2nd Series	1934	70.00	35.00
1351	50	Arms of the Bishopric	1907	90.00	40.00

A SELECTION FROM WILLS

SET No: 166

SET No: 69

SET No: 351

SET No: 1349

SET No: 631

SET No: 387

SET No: 174

SET No: 317

Ref. No.	No. in Set	Name of Set	Date	COMPLETE SETS Grade 1	Grade 2

W. D. & H. O. WILLS LTD. (Cont'd)

Ref. No.	No. in Set	Name of Set	Date	Grade 1	Grade 2
18	50	Arms of the British Empire	1910	70.00	30.00
1780	L25	Arms of the British Empire 1st Series	1931	68.00	38.00
1781	L25	Arms of the British Empire 2nd Series	1932	68.00	38.00
1143	L25	Arms of Universities	1923	64.00	32.00
37	50	Association Footballers (Frame on Back)	1935	80.00	40.00
69	50	Association Footballers (No Frame on Back)	1939	90.00	45.00
793	50	Association Footballers (Eire — non-adhesive) A.A.	1939	120.00	60.00
1782	L25	Auction Bridge	1926	100.00	50.00
166	50	Aviation	1910	140.00	65.00
	?100	Beauties, Collotype	1895	—	—
	52	Beauties (Playing card insets brown backs)	1897	2000.00	1000.00
	K52	Beauties (Playing card insets grey backs)	1896	2400.00	1200.00
1144	L25	Beautiful Homes	1930	100.00	50.00
630	48	Between Two Fires (Sect.)	1930	22.00	11.00
1207	50	Billiards	1909	120.00	60.00
	K9	Boer War Medallions (Brass Medallions)	1901	1050.00	525.00
	50	Borough Arms (Scroll back, Numbered)	1904	850.00	425.00
1349	50	Borough Arms (Scroll back, Unnumbered) A.A.	1904	106.00	48.00
1348	50	Borough Arms 1st (1-50) A.A.	1904	95.00	45.00
172	50	Borough Arms 2nd Edition (1-50) A.A.	1906	65.00	30.00
168	50	Borough Arms 2nd Series (51-100)	1904	65.00	30.00
1347	50	Borough Arms 2nd Edition (51-100) A.A.	1906	65.00	30.00
1350	50	Borough Arms 3rd Series (101-150 Red Print)	1905	65.00	30.00
1344	50	Borough Arms 3rd Series (101-150 Grey Print) A.A.	1905	90.00	40.00
1346	50	Borough Arms 2nd Edition (101-150) A.A.	1906	65.00	30.00
174	50	Borough Arms 4th Series (151-200)	1905	65.00	30.00
351	24	Britain's Part in the War	1917	48.00	22.00
631	50	British Birds	1917	95.00	45.00
387	50	British Butterflies	1927	70.00	35.00
236	L25	British Castles	1925	100.00	50.00
1145	L25	British School of Painting	1927	60.00	30.00
1146	M48	British Sporting Personalities	1927	60.00	30.00
1596	50	Builders of the Empire	1898	520.00	260.00
648	L40	Butterflies & Moths	1938	50.00	25.00
3112	1	Calendar for 1911	1910	24.00	12.00

COMPLETE SETS

Ref. No.	No. in Set	Name of Set	Date	Grade 1	Grade 2
		W. D. & H. O. WILLS LTD. (Cont'd)			
3901	1	Calendar for 1912	1911	15.00	7.50
1889	L25	Cathedrals	1933	98.00	48.00
1559	L25	Celebrated Pictures 1st Series	1916	80.00	40.00
1165	L25	Celebrated Pictures 2nd Series	1916	100.00	50.00
167	50	Celebrated Ships	1911	95.00	45.00
520	25	Cinema Stars 1st Series	1928	64.00	32.00
521	25	Cinema Stars 2nd Series	1928	52.00	26.00
518	50	Cinema Stars 3rd Series	1931	140.00	70.00
120	P12	Cities of Britain	1929	150.00	75.00
	25	Conundrums	1898	350.00	175.00
	25	Conundrums (with album clause) A.A.	1898	260.00	130.00
	60	Coronation Ser. (backs — narrow arrows)	1902	600.00	300.00
1353	60	Coronation Ser. (backs — wide arrows) A.A.	1902	500.00	250.00
	50	Cricketers	1896	5800.00	2800.00
1354	50	Cricketers	1901	1900.00	950.00
354	50	Cricketers (WILL's)	1908	460.00	230.00
1798	25	Cricketers (WILL'S) A.A.	1908	290.00	130.00
352	50	Cricketers 1928	1928	120.00	60.00
353	50	Cricketers 2nd Series	1929	100.00	50.00
63	50	Dogs	1937	48.00	24.00
795	50	Dogs (Eire — non-adhesive) A.A.	1937	110.00	55.00
1148	L25	Dogs 1st Series	1914	150.00	75.00
1149	L25	Dogs 2nd Series	1915	150.00	75.00
1924	50	Double Meaning (Without P/C Inset)	1898	900.00	450.00
121	52	Double Meaning (With P/C Inset) I.A.	1898	1000.00	500.00
234	50	Do You Know? 1st Series	1922	36.00	18.00
53	50	Do You Know? 2nd Series	1924	28.00	14.00
370	50	Do You Know? 3rd Series	1926	28.00	14.00
498	50	Do You Know? 4th Series	1933	36.00	18.00
199	50	Engineering Wonders	1927	32.00	16.00
523	50	English Period Costumes	1929	80.00	40.00
1306	L25	English Period Costumes (Different)	1927	120.00	60.00
	P48	Familiar Phrases (Embassy)	1986	40.00	—
1150	L40	Famous British Authors	1937	90.00	45.00
392	L30	Famous British Liners 1st Series	1934	200.00	100.00
1455	L30	Famous British Liners 2nd Series	1935	144.00	72.00
339	L25	Famous Golfers	1930	550.00	275.00
235	50	Famous Inventions	1915	85.00	40.00
581	50	First Aid (No album clause)	1913	90.00	45.00
220	50	First Aid (With album clause) A.A.	1915	90.00	45.00
1208	50	Fish and Bait	1910	140.00	65.00

Ref. No.	No. in Set	Name of Set	Date	Grade 1	Grade 2
		COMPLETE SETS			
		W. D. & H. O. WILLS LTD. (Cont'd)			
394	25	Flags of the Empire 1st Series	1926	50.00	25.00
393	25	Flags of the Empire 2nd Series	1929	50.00	25.00
264	50	Flower Culture in Pots	1925	30.00	15.00
1151	L30	Flowering Shrubs	1935	56.00	28.00
54	50	Flowering Trees & Shrubs	1924	52.00	26.00
	66	Football Series	1902	660.00	330.00
3	50	Garden Flowers	1933	40.00	20.00
67	50	Garden Flowers by Sudell	1939	18.00	9.00
	50	Garden Flowers by Sudell (Eire) A.A.	1939	28.00	14.00
649	L40	Garden Flowers — New Varieties 1st Series	1938	32.00	16.00
650	L40	Garden Flowers — New Varieties 2nd Series	1939	28.00	14.00
61	50	Garden Hints	1938	16.00	8.00
	50	Garden Hints (Eire) A.A.	1938	24.00	12.00
263	50	Gardening Hints	1923	24.00	12.00
184	50	Garden Life	1914	55.00	25.00
219	50	Gems of Belgian Architecture	1915	65.00	30.00
1211	50	Gems of French Architecture	1917	120.00	55.00
1355	50	Gems of Russian Architecture	1916	65.00	30.00
1302	L25	Golfing	1924	320.00	160.00
	X32	Happy Families	1939	260.00	130.00
1785	L25	Heraldic Signs & Their Origin	1925	90.00	45.00
175	50	Historic Events	1912	95.00	45.00
176	54	Homeland Events (F)	1932	15.00	10.00
260	50	Household Hints	1927	24.00	12.00
666	50	Household Hints 2nd Series	1930	36.00	18.00
65	50	Household Hints (Different)	1936	14.00	7.00
4184	50	Hurlers (Eire)	1927	110.00	55.00
148	P12	Industries of Britain	1930	150.00	75.00
149	25	Irish Beauty Spots	1929	200.00	100.00
150	25	Irish Holiday Resorts	1930	200.00	100.00
3486	50	Irish Industries	1937	80.00	40.00
151	25	Irish Rugby Internationals	1928	300.00	150.00
4185	50	Irish Sportsmen	1935	260.00	130.00
1356	50	Kings & Queens (Short card Grey back)	1897	480.00	230.00
	50	Kings & Queens (Short card Brown back)	1898	960.00	460.00
	51	Kings & Queens (Long Card)	1902	530.00	250.00
332	L25	Lawn Tennis	1931	230.00	115.00
1893	50	Life in the Hedgerow	Unissued	25.00	—
68	50	Life in the Royal Navy	1939	22.00	11.00
194	50	Life in the Treetops	1925	26.00	13.00

SET No: 175

SET No: 152

SET No: 68

SET No: 1359

SET No: 194

SET No: 210

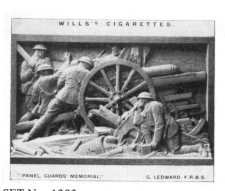

SET No: 1303

Ref. No.	No. in Set	Name of Set	Date	COMPLETE SETS Grade 1	Grade 2

W. D. & H. O. WILLS LTD. (Cont'd)

Ref. No.	No. in Set	Name of Set	Date	Grade 1	Grade 2
1358	50	Locomotives & Rolling Stock (No clause)	1901	700.00	300.00
152	50	Locomotives & Rolling Stock (I.T.C. clause) A.A.	1902	700.00	300.00
862	7	Locomotives & Rolling Stock (7 additional cards)	1901	300.00	150.00
214	50	Lucky Charms	1923	24.00	12.00
563	50	Medals	1906	200.00	100.00
52	50	Merchant Ships of the World	1924	84.00	42.00
1359	50	Military Motors (Passed by censor)	1916	150.00	65.00
582	50	Military Motors (Not passed by censor) A.A.	1916	150.00	65.00
153	52	Miniature Playing Cards (Blue back, Nd.)	1932	35.00	20.00
	52	Miniature Playing Cards (Blue back, Unnumbered) A.A.	1932	35.00	20.00
	52	Miniature Playing Cards (Blue back, Red overprints) A.A.	1934	35.00	20.00
	52	Miniature Playing Cards (Pink back) A.A.	1932	40.00	26.00
	52	Miniature Playing Cards (Pink back, Red overprints) A.A.	1934	40.00	26.00
291	50	Mining	1916	100.00	50.00
3771	L25	Modern Architecture	1931	60.00	30.00
1303	L30	Modern British Sculpture	1928	70.00	35.00
1265	48	Mother & Son (Sect.)	1931	21.00	10.50
210	50	Musical Celebrities 1st Series	1911	250.00	110.00
1212	50	Musical Celebrities 2nd Series	1916	350.00	160.00
	8	Original cards withdrawn from above set	1916	—	—
	25	National Costumes	1895	8400.00	4200.00
451	50	Naval Dress & Badges	1909	205.00	95.00
395	50	Nelson Series	1905	290.00	135.00
292	50	Old English Garden Flowers 1st Series	1910	65.00	30.00
293	50	Old English Garden Flowers 2nd Series	1913	65.00	30.00
1154	L25	Old Furniture 1st Series	1923	150.00	75.00
1155	L25	Old Furniture 2nd Series	1924	150.00	75.00
331	L40	Old Inns 1st Series	1936	180.00	90.00
335	L40	Old Inns 2nd Series	1939	96.00	48.00
1304	L25	Old London	1929	160.00	80.00
1834	L30	Old Pottery & Porcelain	1934	60.00	30.00
1156	L25	Old Silver	1924	120.00	60.00
1305	L25	Old Sundials	1938	110.00	55.00
	20	Our Gallant Grenadiers	1902	1040.00	520.00
196	50	Our King & Queen	1937	18.00	9.00
217	50	Overseas Dominions — Australia	1915	55.00	25.00
218	50	Overseas Dominions — Canada	1914	55.00	25.00

SET No: 218

SET No: 1659

SET No: 64

SET No: 1154

SET No: 293

SET No: 294

SET No: 1845

Ref. No.	No. in Set	Name of Set	Date	COMPLETE SETS Grade 1	Grade 2
		W. D. & H. O. WILLS LTD. (Cont'd)			
294	50	Physical Culture	1914	75.00	35.00
	D5	Pica Punchline	1984	5.00	—
2129	25	Pond & Aquarium 1st Series	Unissued	8.00	—
3615	25	Pond & Aquarium 2nd Series	Unissued	10.00	—
886	50	Portraits of European Royalty (1-50)	1908	110.00	50.00
887	50	Portraits of European Royalty (51-100)	1908	130.00	60.00
1157	L25	Public Schools	1927	120.00	60.00
1158	L25	Punch Cartoons 1st Series	1916	160.00	80.00
	L25	Punch Cartoons 2nd Series	1917	750.00	350.00
	L144	Punch Lines (Embassy)	1983	60.00	—
	D288	Punch Lines (Embassy)	1983	120.00	—
	40	Puppies	Unissued	—	—
1159	L40	Racehorses & Jockeys	1938	110.00	55.00
209	50	Radio Celebrities 1st Series	1934	60.00	30.00
	50	Radio Celebrities A Series (Eire) A.A.	1934	80.00	40.00
10	50	Radio Celebrities 2nd Series	1935	44.00	22.00
	50	Radio Celebrities 2nd Series (Eire) A.A.	1935	80.00	40.00
215	50	Railway Engines	1924	100.00	50.00
8	50	Railway Engines	1936	80.00	40.00
	50	Railway Engines (Eire) A.A.	1936	130.00	65.00
62	50	Railway Equipment	1939	20.00	10.00
550	50	Railway Locomotives	1930	120.00	60.00
647	12	Recruiting Posters	1915	180.00	80.00
2780	L25	Rigs of Ships	1929	150.00	75.00
	D48	Ring the Changes	1985	32.00	—
237	50	Romance of the Heavens	1928	32.00	16.00
261	50	Roses 1st Series	1912	90.00	40.00
262	50	Roses 2nd Series	1913	80.00	35.00
204	50	Roses (Different)	1926	56.00	28.00
1161	L40	Roses (Different)	1936	60.00	30.00
1160	M48	Round Europe	1937	20.00	10.00
1214	50	Rugby Internationals	1929	96.00	48.00
9	50	Safety First	1934	80.00	40.00
	50	Safety First (Eire) A.A.	1934	120.00	60.00
1360	50	School Arms	1906	65.00	30.00
1659	50	Seaside Resorts	1899	800.00	400.00
3651	40	Shannon Electric Power Scheme	1931	100.00	50.00
	25	Ships (Grey Star & Circle)	1895	1300.00	650.00
	25	Ships (Three Castles back) A.A.	1895	1300.00	650.00
873	50	Ships (Wills on front) Grey back	1896	1600.00	800.00
1961	100	Ships (Brown back) (Including above 2 sets)	1898	3200.00	1600.00
212	50	Ships Badges	1925	36.00	18.00

A SELECTION OF FILM STAR SETS

CARRERAS
SET 403

CARRERAS
SET 594

CARRERAS
SET 1234

PLAYER SET 1131

CARRERAS SET 1178

CARRERAS SET 2054

CARRERAS SET 657

**COMPLETE
SETS**

Ref. No.	No. in Set	Name of Set	Date	Grade 1	Grade 2
		W. D. & H. O. WILLS LTD. (Cont'd)			
1361	50	Signalling Series	1911	86.00	36.00
1848	50	Soldiers and Sailors (Blue back)	1896	4000.00	2000.00
	50	Soldiers & Sailors (Grey back) A.A.	1896	4000.00	2000.00
1845	100	Soldiers of the World (Ltd. back)	1895	1400.00	700.00
	100	Soldiers of the World (Without Ltd. back) A.A.	1896	1100.00	550.00
	1	England, Drummer Boy (Additional card to above set)	1896	180.00	90.00
	52	Soldiers of the World (with P/C insert)	1896	2200.00	1100.00
396	50	Speed	1930	110.00	55.00
64	50	Speed (Different)	1938	24.00	12.00
	50	Speed (Eire)	1938	60.00	30.00
1529	50	Sport of all Nations	1900	750.00	350.00
536	50	Strange Craft	1931	98.00	48.00
1415	48	The Boyhood of Raleigh (Sect.)	1930	24.00	12.00
154	P12	The British Empire	1929	144.00	72.00
467	50	The Coronation Series	1911	96.00	48.00
1162	L40	The King's Art Treasures	1938	20.00	10.00
1263	48	The Laughing Cavalier (Sect.) Series No. 5	1931	24.00	12.00
	48	The Laughing Cavalier (Sect. Eire — Series No. 2) A.A.	1931	150.00	75.00
	50	The Life of H.M. King Edward VIII	Unissued	—	—
5	50	The Reign of King George V	1935	48.00	24.00
195	50	The Sea Shore	1938	20.00	10.00
796	50	The Sea Shore (Eire — non-adhesive) A.A.	1938	56.00	28.00
1264	48	The Toast (Sect.) Series No. 4	1931	20.00	10.00
	48	The Toast (Sect. Eire — Series No. 1) A.A.	1931	150.00	75.00
213	25	The World's Dreadnoughts	1910	110.00	50.00
1362	50	Time & Money	1906	130.00	65.00
3136	50	Transvaal Series (Black Border)	1899	750.00	375.00
2882	66	Transvaal Series (White Border)	1900	200.00	100.00
2883	66	Transvaal Series (Capstan back)	1902	550.00	275.00
1163	L40	Trees	1937	60.00	30.00
3155	L25	University Hoods & Gowns	1926	110.00	55.00
1599	50	Vanity Fair (Unnumbered)	1902	450.00	225.00
1598	50	Vanity Fair 1st Series	1902	450.00	225.00
1527	50	Vanity Fair 2nd Series	1902	450.00	225.00
	50	Waterloo	Unissued	—	—
2474	50	Wild Animals of the World (Green scroll back)	1900	400.00	200.00

A SELECTION OF HORSERACING SETS

SET 1159

SET 485

SET 5526

SET 600

SET 3141

SET 1480

SET 509

GALLAHER SET 95

Ref. No.	No. in Set	Name of Set	Date	Grade 1	Grade 2
		COMPLETE SETS			
		W. D. & H. O. WILLS LTD. (Cont'd)			
3123	52	Wild Animals of the World (Grey back P/C Inset)	1900	1100.00	510.00
198	50	Wild Flowers	1923	40.00	20.00
173	50	Wild Flowers 1st Series	1936	24.00	12.00
	50	Wild Flowers (Eire) A.A.	1936	50.00	25.00
46	50	Wild Flowers 2nd Series	1937	18.00	9.00
798	50	Wild Flowers 2nd Series (Eire — non-adhesive)	1937	50.00	25.00
456	50	Wonders of the Past	1926	40.00	20.00
230	50	Wonders of the Sea	1928	40.00	20.00
727	M36	World of Firearms (Embassy Cigars)	1982	5.00	—
728	M36	World of Speed (Embassy Cigars)	1981	5.00	—
		J. WIX & SONS LTD.			
	?1	Animals (Australasian Issue) (F)	1929	60.00	30.00
	P80	Bridge Favours & Place Cards	1937	1100.00	700.00
	P50	Bridge Hands	1937	850.00	550.00
832	L48	British Empire Flags (Silk)	1938	80.00	40.00
765	L48	British Empire Flags (Silk, Printed in U.S.A.) A.A.	1938	80.00	40.00
127	50	Builders of Empire	1937	28.00	14.00
699	42	Card Tricks by Jasper Maskelyne	1938	150.00	100.00
	M42	Card Tricks by Jasper Maskelyne	1938	150.00	100.00
1290	50	Coronation (Kensitas back)	1937	22.00	11.00
766	50	Coronation (Wix back — Linen front) A.A.	1937	22.00	11.00
767	50	Coronation (Wix back — Varnished front) A.A.	1937	22.00	11.00
1200	L50	Henry	1935	48.00	24.00
1204	P25	Henry A.A.	1935	110.00	55.00
1201	L50	Henry, 2nd Series	1936	90.00	45.00
4137	P25	Henry, 2nd Series A.A.	1936	140.00	70.00
1570	L50	Henry, 3rd Series	1936	44.00	22.00
1571	L50	Henry, 4th Series	1936	44.00	22.00
2063	L50	Henry, 5th Series	1937	44.00	22.00
	L?160	Jenkynisms (Yellow Card)	1932	170.00	110.00
	?145	Jenkynisms (Red Borders on paper)	1931	—	—
	L?145	Jenkynisms (Red Borders on paper)	1931	—	—
3390	P12	Ken-Cards Series 1. Starters/Snacks	1969	6.00	4.00
3391	P12	Ken-Cards Series 2. Main Courses	1969	6.00	4.00

SET No: 127

SET No: 699

SET No: 2063

SET No: 3665

SET No: 1290

SET No: 698

**COMPLETE
SETS**

Ref. No.	No. in Set	Name of Set	Date	Grade 1	Grade 2
		J. WIX & SONS LTD. (Cont'd)			
3392	P12	Ken-Cards Series 3. Desserts	1969	6.00	4.00
3393	P12	Ken-Cards Series 4. Motoring	1969	6.00	4.00
3394	P12	Ken-Cards Series 5. Gardening	1970	6.00	4.00
3395	P12	Ken-Cards Series 6. Do It Yourself	1970	6.00	4.00
3396	P12	Ken-Cards Series 7. Home Hints	1970	6.00	4.00
3397	P12	Ken-Cards Series 8. Fishing	1970	6.00	4.00
1944	60	Kensitas Flowers (Woven Silks — Plain back)	1934	320.00	160.00
768	60	Kensitas Flowers (Woven Silks — Printed back) A.A.	1934	320.00	160.00
1945	L60	Kensitas Flowers (Woven Silks — Plain back) A.A.	1934	480.00	240.00
769	L60	Kensitas Flowers (Woven Silks — Printed back) A.A.	1934	480.00	240.00
3216	P30	Kensitas Flowers (Woven Silks — Plain back)	1934	2200.00	1100.00
	P30	Kensitas Flowers (Woven Silks — Printed back) A.A.	1934	2200.00	1100.00
1942	40	Kensitas Flowers 2nd Series (Woven Silks)	1935	600.00	300.00
1943	L40	Kensitas Flowers 2nd Series (Woven Silks) A.A.	1935	800.00	400.00
889	25	Love Scenes from Famous Films 1st Series	1932	120.00	60.00
812	L25	Love Scenes from Famous Films 1st Series	1932	120.00	60.00
	P25	Love Scenes from Famous Films 1st Series	1932	180.00	90.00
698	25	Love Scenes from Famous Films 2nd Series	1932	120.00	60.00
	L25	Love Scenes from Famous Films 2nd Series	1932	160.00	80.00
	P25	Love Scenes from Famous Films 2nd Series	1932	330.00	165.00
2595	K53	Miniature Playing Cards (Blue Scroll)	1938	16.00	8.00
5245	K53	Miniature Playing Cards (Red Scroll)	1938	16.00	8.00
5418	K53	Miniature Playing Cards (Drake's "Revenge")	1938	20.00	10.00
5419	K53	Miniature Playing Cards (Nelson's "Victory")	1938	20.00	10.00
651	L60	National Flags (Silk)	1939	100.00	50.00

A SELECTION OF RAILWAY SETS

SET 1110

SET 550

PATTREIOUEX SET 72

PATTREIOUEX SET 2483

SET 1358

SET 152

SET 3789

SET 1477

SET 122

Details of Grading on Page 5.

Ref. No.	No. in Set	Name of Set	Date	COMPLETE SETS Grade 1	Grade 2
		J. WIX & SONS LTD. (Cont'd)			
	24	Royal Tour of New Zealand (N.Z. Issue) (F)	1928	250.00	125.00
3316	25	Scenes from Famous Films (Third Series)	1933	120.00	60.00
3315	P25	Scenes from Famous Films (Third Series)	1933	280.00	140.00
		JOHN J. WOODS			
	?12	Views of London	1905	3000.00	1500.00
		T. WOOD & SONS			
	30	Army Pictures, Cartoons, etc.	1916	3800.00	1900.00
		WOOD BROS.			
	28	Dominoes	1912	2600.00	1300.00
		W. H. & J. WOODS LTD.			
2079	25	Aesop's Fables	1932	80.00	40.00
3325	50	Modern Motor Cars (F)	1933	350.00	175.00
2080	25	Romance of the Royal Mail	1931	50.00	25.00
876	25	Types of Volunteers & Yeomanry	1901	1300.00	650.00
		J. & E. WOOLFE			
	?50	Beauties (KEWA I)	1900	—	—
		M. H. WOOLLER			
	24	Beauties (BOCCA)	1900	—	—

Continued from page 7

The most ruthless tycoon to emerge in the tobacco industry in America of the 1880s was James B. Duke, and in 1890 he formed the American Tobacco Company from the then five largest tobacco companies in America. From humble beginnings of peddling tobacco around on a cart – and that is really getting in on the ground floor! – he moved on to control the tobacco business in America, and is attributed to have driven out of business or absorbed somewhere in the region of two hundred and fifty firms by 1901.

He set about things in the no-nonsense way that was characteristic of him, but he was more than just another hard-nosed businessman, out for a quick profit. He was responsible for producing beautiful sets of cards, and it is widely believed that the high standard of these played a large part in his success.

Once having control of the American market, Duke had his sights set on the British market as well. The story goes that in September 1901 he disembarked from a ship at Liverpool, marched straight into the factory of Ogdens Ltd., and bought them out, lock, stock and barrel. They must have wondered just what had hit them.

He set about issuing vast amounts of Tabs and Guinea Gold cards. These were photographic cards of politicians, actresses and various events of the times, and as photography was in its infancy at that period they were obviously very popular. It is generally believed that the cards cost more to produce than did the cigarettes themselves, and just to illustrate the smoothness of Mr. James B. Duke, he bought back the cards from the public, mounted them in special albums and presented them to hospitals, free of cost.

By now he had the 'big guns' firmly trained on the British market, and so intense was the competition between Britain and America that from the period 1900–1902 there raged what was to become known as 'The Tobacco War'. Duke was obviously a force to be reckoned with and buying out Ogdens must have seemed like the last straw as far as his competitors were concerned.

On the 2nd November 1901 Britain launched her counter-attack. Wills and twelve other companies formed the Imperial Tobacco Company to combat the American Tobacco Company. Vast amounts of cigarette cards were 'fired' in all directions, but inevitably the battle became too costly for all parties concerned and an armistice was declared. Then they all put their heads together and divided up the battleground. Ogdens was 'repatriated' by the Imperial Tobacco Company who would control the British market. The American Tobacco Company would control America and Cuba, and the newly-formed British-American Tobacco Company (B.A.T.) would handle the other overseas interests.

The earliest British cigarette cards were believed to be the advertisement cards appearing in the late 1880s, but by the end of the Tobacco War sets were appearing in all major brands in this country at regular intervals. This was to continue up until the end of the First World War when a paper shortage imposed its own restrictions.

After a brief lapse cigarette cards re-emerged. To begin with they were mostly re-issues of sets in circulation before the First World War. But as cigarette cards became more popular, inevitably, new sets began to emerge, and by 1930 the hobby was stronger than ever. Many dealers had set up in business and societies and clubs were formed throughout the country.

The thirties were generally known as the heyday of cigarette cards, with large amounts of cards and sets being produced by all major firms. The hobby was becoming still more organized, with reference books and magazines being produced. It took the Second World War to, once again, bring cigarette cards to a halt, as they were ceased, due to the inevitable paper shortage. Sad to say, with the end of the war they were not to re-emerge with the same zeal as before.

Throughout the forties and fifties Carreras continued to produce sets with their packets of Turf cigarettes, but these were nowhere near as popular as the pre-war issues, as due to various regulations they were not printed in colour, and for economic reasons were printed on the inside of the packets.

In the fifties and sixties the Amalgamated Tobacco Corporation issued a number of sets in the Channel Islands, but again the printing was not up to the previous standards. In the sixties Player's, Churchman's and various other manufacturers produced a number of sets which, for some unknown reason, were never issued. In 1976 Carreras again began re-issuing sets of cards with their Black Cat cigarettes. But the trend in the last few years is more towards cards being issued with cigars rather than cigarettes.

How, some may ask, has the result of cigarette cards not being issued in very large amounts effected the hobby in recent years? We can only answer that since 1970 cigarette card collecting has been rapidly on the increase, going from strength to strength, and many veteran collectors tell me that cartophily is more popular now than it has ever been before. There are more articles to be found in publications on the bookstalls, better catalogues and more enthusiasm than ever, and the magic appeal of cigarette cards lives on.

(III)

COLLECTING FOR PLEASURE AND INVESTMENT

But now to the business of what you are really interested in. The actual collecting of cigarette cards and how to go about it. To get the best from cigarette card collecting you need only to follow a few simple basic rules. First and foremost, to collect what appeals to you personally. There is little use in building up a collection of unattractive cards on subjects which have no interest to you. This may sound somewhat elementary but I have seen it done on many occasions.

Secondly, it is as well to decide on the standard of condition concerning the cards to be collected, remembering that to collect willy-nilly any old rubbish that comes along may at first seem all very well, but should you, at some later date, decide to sell your collection, you may well be in for a disappointment. We would suggest a minimum of good collectable grade 2 sets. If one sets too high a standard and accepts only grade 1 sets, this will, of course, impose severe restrictions as they are becoming more difficult to obtain all the time. Most of today's collectors settle for a happy medium, and whereas they would obviously all prefer mint condition sets, their collections will contain sets in grade 2 condition.

A third factor to bear in mind is that if you have incomplete sets or odd cards, these will never realize the same kind of value as a complete set, so wherever possible keep to buying sets. As always there is an exception to the rule, and this is the very rare cards which are virtually unobtainable more than one or two odd cards at a time.

Another pitfall to steer clear of is sending through the post for cards from strangers. Bidding blind at auctions without seeing the cards first should also be avoided, unless you are familiar with the auctioneers' system of grading condition. Cigarette cards are becoming increasingly hard to find and some auction lots *are* virtually junk which no one wants, either poor condition or not very collectable cards. However, collectors can often secure a bargain at auctions and come across scarce sets and rare part sets and odd cards that are virtually impossible to find in their set form. But although the auction has become part of the cigarette card scene, new collectors are advised to tread very carefully unless they can trust the advice of the auctioneer. Details of our own Auctions can be found on page 8.

Another method of seeking out cigarette cards is to prowl around antique and second-hand shops. With regard to the former, if it is a well established place they will most likely be 'in the know' as far as the value of any cards that they may have in stock are concerned. For, it is their business to be well informed on anything, be it coins, paintings, furniture or cigarette cards.

But regarding the other shops, you may well unearth some very pleasant surprises. There are many such places nowadays, operating on short-term leases in areas that are due for redevelopment. These particular places (often unkindly referred to as junk shops) are usually charity shops such as Oxfam, and they stock all manner of objects. It is well worth having a poke around these places, for some fine treasures can be discovered in that little 'junk shop' down the road. Also a great deal of fun can be derived from this. The thought that maybe . . . maybe I'll come across one of those Clarke's 'Tobacco Leaf Girls', for example, can add spice to the business. The 'hunt and the kill' element that any collector appreciates.

Even so, you would be flying blind without some form of reference book to aid you in your searches, so always remember to take your catalogue with you. This gives you an up to date guide as to today's values and enables you to decide for yourself whether or not you are getting a bargain.

There are certain points, though, to bear in mind, and one in particular cannot be stressed too often. The condition of the cards is very important, and if your catalogue states that a grade two set is worth £5.00 it is no bargain to buy a dog-eared, dirty set for £2.00. Please remember we are always willing to buy good collectable to mint condition sets, whereas we are not interested in soiled or damaged cards.

As a collector you will find that a visit to our shop is well worthwhile. If you are a new collector you will probably be unfamiliar with most of the series, and our display albums enable you to browse through the sets so that you can see exactly what you are buying. There is always someone available to advise you on the best method of housing your cards etc. Most new collectors have a few questions to ask which we are only too pleased to answer. The more experienced collector will also find items of interest, and we can usually be relied upon to dig out a few surprises – even for the long-in-the-tooth cigarette card buff. We have a good name to live up to and we are always willing to offer our customers any advice they may require.

But whether you are buying or selling we always offer collectors a fair deal. We have customers from all corners of the world and our knowledge of this particular market guarantees that you will get value for money.

Like everything it must be realized that there is a difference between the price at which you sell your cards and that which you pay for them. The business of dealing in cigarette cards is far more complex than most people realize. As well as the usual overheads of rent, rates, telephone, electricity, staff etc., there are the additional costs of advertising and producing publications such as this. There are also many hidden factors. Few people are aware that cigarette cards stored in bulk need to be kept at room temperature. There is also the expense of insurance and security, not to mention the upkeep of our business premises.

The mail order section of our business is also more complicated than generally realized, involving adding, franking and addressing machines, typewriters and so forth, all of which have to be supplied and maintained.

There is a great deal of behind-the-scenes activity, too, sorting out the collections and banding up the sets suitable for stock. We are by no means complaining, but merely pointing out that when one sells their cards, business overheads have to be taken into consideration.

One has only to glance through the pages of this catalogue to see that the prices of cigarette cards varies tremendously. These prices are based realistically on a number of factors. The first factor is, of course, the rarity of the card. If a set of cards was produced in very large amounts it is obviously not going to be as valuable as a set of which there may only be a few in existence.

The second factor which is equally as important as the first, is the condition of the cards. Poor condition cards are virtually worthless, therefore, we advise collecting a minimum of good collectable condition sets (Grade 2).

Sets which are excellent to mint (Grade 1) will obviously cost more, but experienced collectors invariably consider the extra expense a wise investment.

Subject matter should also be taken into consideration. The cards cover virtually every topic in the alphabet from Astrology to Zoology. The trick is to know which are the most popular and therefore easily resaleable.

The fact that cigarette cards are not overpriced came through loud and clear through the recent recession when each year they continued to rise in value, whereas there was a sharp drop in the value of stamps and various other collectables. We consider that the main contributory factor to this is that the majority of people who collect cigarette cards do so simply because they want to, with the investment side of it as a secondary consideration. But inevitably, when a collector has built up a reasonable size collection he will find himself in the position of an investor, even though this was probably not his original intention. It therefore follows, and only makes sense, that before one starts collecting it is as well to consider the few simple rules that we have outlined.

There is a great deal of pleasure to be derived from building up a good collection, apart from the initial thrill of actually collecting the cards, your collection will prove to be a unique set of reference books on your favourite subjects. With artistic pictures on the front and interesting texts on the back, what more can one ask from a hobby?

The prices in our catalogue are, of course, accepted for insurance purposes. Details of insurance can be obtained through ourselves or you can approach your own insurance company or brokers.

As cigarette cards have increased in value at a steady pace over the years the wise collector is the one who buys sets in the right condition which appeal to him, and in all possibility he will see his collection increase in value in the years to come. But it would be foolish indeed to think that to buy cigarette cards today and sell them in the space of a few months would bring in a large profit. We have, however, in the past, had many customers who had purchased cigarette cards from us then sold the same sets back to us a few years later for an appreciably higher price than they had originally paid us for them.

(IV)

CIGARETTE CARDS OF OTHER COUNTRIES

Though the aim of most collectors is to collect sets of cigarette cards issued in the United Kingdom, there are many who desire to add some of the better foreign sets to their treasure trove. But generally speaking many of the overseas issues are not regarded as being particularly collectable. One glaring reason being that the text on the back is often in a foreign language, and this can prove very frustrating to the industrious collector who has acquired a set on a subject that may be of great interest to him, only to come up against the previous mentioned and maddening enigma.

One particular instance springs to mind concerning a customer of ours who obtained a set of Chinese cards. Now we all can appreciate his problem, knowing what Chinese writing looks like. Undaunted by this he hit upon the ideal solution. He took the cards to his local Chinese 'take-away' to have them translated. Unfortunately the proprietor was an astute man of business and the ways of the world in general, and he duly obliged with the translation — one card at a time! The poor chap who owned the cards has not been able to bear the sight of Chinese food since — his scheme evidently cost him dear in Chinese 'take-aways' before he managed to get the whole set translated. So let that be a warning to you. Fiendishly cunning, these Orientals!

Sets have also been issued in French, Arabic, Greek, Dutch, Siamese, Flemish, Italian, Norwegian and German among many other languages. Japan did not issue a great quantity, though their Match Box series were printed in vast numbers. One would have expected Japan to have led the international field in such a lucrative enterprise in much the same sort of highly competitive way as they do nowadays. Could the reason have been that plastic, not having been invented in those days, had something to do with it?

Most collectors would probably agree that many of the most distinctive overseas cards ever issued were the early American cards from 1880 to the turn of the century. Sad to say, they are very difficult to obtain in the right condition as, in those earlier days, it was the custom of American collectors to stick them in scrapbooks, thus damaging the backs.

Malta produced many cards but they have little if any collecting value. Many of them are black and white photographs of views, statues, monuments and out-of-date politicians. Their sets of Nelson, Wellington and Napoleon are among their most collectable.

Most overseas cards with English text were issued by the American Tobacco Co. (A.T.C.) or the British American Tobacco Co. (B.A.T.). In the case of the latter the majority of their sets were also issued in this country with U.K. brands, however, to make things more confusing some of the names of B.A.T. sets do not correspond with the U.K. sets, for instance B.A.T. "Butterflies" is completely different to Players "Butterflies", whereas B.A.T. "Aeroplanes of Today" is the same set as Players "Aeroplanes Civil". Many of the B.A.T. sets were issued with a plain back which are never popular with collectors, others known as anonymous cards were issued with no maker's name or brand of cigarettes on the back. However, some A.T.C. and B.A.T. sets which are both attractive and different to those issued in the U.K. are very collectable.

Australia and New Zealand, too, issued a good number of sets, though many of the Wills issues were identical to those issued in the United Kingdom.

Canadian sets were, like those of Australia and New Zealand, much the same as those issued here, though happily, yet again, there are exceptions.

South Africa produced its fair quota, the text on most sets being both in English and Afrikaan, but once again their cards are not particularly sought after, owing to their poor printing and rather unimaginative subjects. There are exceptions, of course, such as the various sports sets.

South America was not to be left out either. Most of their cards were of a somewhat risque nature, a sort of 'what the butler saw' type of thing. Some of these sets prove to be quite amusing, though most collectors would be satisfied to have but one or two sets as they tend to become repetitive.

There are some intriguing stories circulating in the cartophilic world concerning the German issues. Evidently Adolf Hitler forbade the issue of cigarette cards in Germany as likely to distract schoolboys from their studies. The story goes that Goebbels pointed out that cards could not only be educational but also a means of winning over popular opinion – in other words, a ready-made propaganda machine.

And so German cards were reprieved, just as long as they 'toed the party line' and did not offend the Führeur's policies. It is difficult to say if this is literally true, though on the other hand it is quite feasible, for the greater percentage of German issues were devoted to supporting the Nazi regime.

One set entitled 'Adolf Hitler' showed that gentleman in the company of Goebbels, Goering and Himmler, patting young children on the head, chatting affably with old folk and visiting the sick in true pre-election canvassing style to show what a jolly good sort he really was!

But in spite of the predominance of military sets there were many other subjects covered by German cards in a large variety of issues.

A number of different sets were issued by Wills in India under their brand name 'Scissors'. These sets are completely different to those issued in the United Kingdom and most of them are indeed very collectable.

Other cigarette cards were also issued in the Far East, but they are, like the curate's egg, only good in parts. Chinese sets tend to tell a story – if you can read Chinese. Remember if you will the collector mentioned earlier and be warned. Siamese sets also tend to have a style of their own and a few sets look fine in a well displayed collection.

But generally speaking, few collectors would have any desire to build up a collection of Far Eastern cards as they tend to be too repetitive. 'Home-grown' issues have always held pride of place to the greater majority of collectors who, if only for nostalgic reasons, prefer to collect sets issued in the United Kingdom.

Collectors who are interested in collecting overseas sets will find a visit to our shop well worthwhile as we always have a selection of overseas sets in stock, many of which have never been catalogued. Alternatively our Postal Auctions are a very useful source of supply.

(V)

MISPRINTS AND VARIATIONS

Series produced in this country can usually be relied upon for accuracy, especially in the years following the First World War, for the producers went to great lengths to ensure that pictures and text were as accurate as possible. Churchman's issued a series of forty cards entitled 'Howlers', but more than enough unintentional howlers were to find their way to the public, despite the vigilance of the manufacturers. For as cigarette cards became part of everyday life, so the gremlins appeared. As with stamps many rarities were due to a simple printing error. Simple maybe, but in many cases hilarious, and cigarette cards were by no means exempt from this phenomenon.

But as far as errors are concerned the attitude between the collectors of cigarette cards and the collectors of stamps varies tremendously. There is no real value attached to error cards. In fact, most collectors would prefer the correct card to the misprinted one.

Player's issued a series entitled 'Dandies', and number 43, Benjamin Disraeli, was a classic example, made even more amusing by the attempts to correct the error. An elegant, twenty-two year-old Disraeli is shown in early Nineteenth Century attire with cane and raised hat. Behind him rises the majestic silhouette of Big

MISPRINTS AND CORRECTIONS

SET 226 PLAYERS "DANDIES"

PLAYERS "CHARACTERS FROM DICKENS"

**CARRERAS SET
617
"FIGURES OF
FICTION"**

WILLS SET 209 "RADIO CELEBRITIES"

Ben — which had not been erected when those clothes were in vogue. Doubtless some exasperated printer argued that the eminent politician may have been wearing an old gardening suit for murky weather, but this would not do. Dandies such as 'Dizzy' wouldn't be seen dead in an out-of-date suit of clothes, so desperate measures — not made-to-measures! — were called for. The card was re-issued with Big Ben erased, but it left a rather ominous smudge that could have been anything. However, it was deemed acceptable for the time being, but later a reprint was issued with only the balustrade in the background behind Disraeli.

One of the 'Radio Celebrities' cards by Wills shows a Captain M.B.T. Wakelam — only it isn't Captain M.B.T. Wakelam! The correction was swiftly dealt with, but whoever the mysterious Mr. X was, it was not revealed. Could it have been the ubiquitous Kilroy?

'Characters from Dickens', by Player's, came up with a real gem. Silas Wegg and his wooden leg. You've guessed it. They chopped the right leg off instead of the left. This was, of course, reprinted. But I think that this was simply done by reversing the print of the drawing as his coat is now buttoned right side over left instead of vice-versa.

And in Carreras 'Characters of Fiction', Uncle Tom (of 'Uncle Tom's Cabin') appeared with a negroid face — but white feet! How about that for racial integration!

There have been instances where a colour has been missed out during the printing process and a card has now and again been found to have a flawless picture on the front but no information on the back, or vice-versa. These last examples are not nearly so interesting or amusing as the actual errors of fact and their corrections.

Apart from errors or misprints there are other cards that, to a certain extent, fall into the category of peculiarities. These are 'varieties', which have been re-issued during the distribution of a set in order to bring it up to date. A classic example would be Wills 'Transvaal' series which was issued at the time of the Boer War. Originally meant to be a series of sixty-six cards, there are no fewer than two-hundred and fifty-seven varieties recorded. Card No. 15 can be Colonel Baden-Powell or Major General Baden-Powell, due to the fortunes of war. Card No. 16, Major General Sir W.P. Symons or the late Major General Sir W.P. Symons (not so fortunate). Promotions and obituaries continued throughout the whole series as the campaign went on.

Collectors who take errors too seriously can easily find themselves very frustrated. Some catalogues in the past have attempted to list cards as being thick or thin cards. This difference could simply have been due to the printer running out of a certain thickness of board and utilizing a thinner one. And a collector attempting to collect cards all of one thickness may find himself coming up against the fact that there are more than two thicknesses involved. Again, simple instances of where a comma may have been missed out are virtually ignored throughout the hobby.

If a set has been printed with two distinct colours of text on the back, i.e. Player's 'Regimental Uniforms' with a blue or a brown back, collectors will normally want all of one of the colours. However, some catalogues have attempted to split hairs to an even finer degree, describing certain other sets as having a light blue or a dark blue back. This again can prove ludicrous, for when laying the cards out together there will be varying shades of blue and it becomes impossible to judge whether they are supposed to be dark or light blue or sky-blue pink. And as the set was never intended to be collected on this basis in the first place the whole exercise becomes futile. Cigarette card collecting should be a relaxing pastime, not a nailbiting ordeal which leads you to a nervous breakdown.

But these errors and misprints cannot be put aside. True, they have only a novelty appeal to collectors, but as far as the manufacturers were concerned a great deal of blood, sweat and tears must have been shed when these 'human fallibilities' came to light. Doubtless there were angry rumblings in high places and someone's head would have rolled, for it is sadly unlikely that the manufacturers would have regarded them in the same good humoured light as collectors do.

(VI)

CIGARETTE CARD NOVELTIES

Some of the early cigarette cards are collectors' items by merit of their design alone. By that I do not mean only the illustrations, but the backs of the cards which were extremely decorative. There are many examples of the most detailed artwork such as scrollwork and other elaborate patterns, all full of intricate detail that is a joy to behold, and it is obvious that the artists took great pride in their work.

Duke, the early American manufacturer, produced some very fine sets of booklets, the most popular of these being 'Histories of Generals', comprising of a set of fifty generals of the time. These were issued about 1880 and are a very attractive set indeed.

Another early oddity were the 'Tobacco Leaf Girls' issued on a card shaped like a tobacco leaf by W.M. Clark & Son. These were issued about 1898 and are very rare and much sought after.

One of the most attractive sets of novelties are a set of twenty-five oval miniatures which are in metal, issued overseas by Wills.

Other notable sets are the woven silks, issued by Wix. These are sets of flowers which were handwoven in the Mediterranean area, presumably as labour was cheaper there. They come in folders, each with a description of the particular flower inserted. This type of card generally comes under the heading of 'silks', although most of the silks are, in fact, printed onto the silk and not woven in. It goes without saying that many of these cards are most attractive, although some of them — flags for example — are inclined to be repetitious. Godfrey Phillips probably issued the largest amount of silk sets, although they were also issued by Anstie, Muratti and many others.

One memorable gimmick used by Player's were transfers. These sets proved to be very popular among children. Indeed, I must own up to the fact that back in the war years (World War II, or course!) when I was at school, we all used to stick them on the back of our hands — much to the disapproval of our teachers who marched us 'grubby little oiks' down to the washrooms to scrub those beloved transfers off. Fortunately most of the Player's transfer sets such as 'Aviary and Cage Birds', 'Butterflies', 'Wild Animal Heads', 'Dogs' etc., were also issued in a very nice card form which are much more collectable and thus preserved for posterity.

Another novel idea were 3D cards which were issued by Godfrey Phillips. These were an extra large size card and it was possible to obtain a pair of green and red spectacles to create the three-dimensional effect. Cavenders also brought out a number of sets of stereoscopic cards, and with these one could obtain a more elaborate metallic viewer which really enhanced the 3D effect.

Another — but not so successful — gimmick were the push-out cards. Ogdens issued a number of these sets. Mitchell's and Cope's also came up with sets of cut-outs, but these sets did not prove to be very popular with collectors, for once they were cut out they were ruined, and in their entire state they are not very attractive.

Not to be at a loss for ideas Cavenders issued black and white views that were actually hand painted.

Carreras launched a set of jig-saw cards called 'Picture Puzzle Series', but sad to say they didn't really have a lot going for them from the collector's point of view as there was little one could do with them except cut them up or leave them . . . or whatever . . .?

In 1924 Godfrey Phillips issued a rather amusing set of novelties. These were puppet like cards of animals etc., which could be manoeuvred to move their eyes and stick their tongues out.

Other manufacturers issued the sectional series. Wills did a number of these which made up into a picture of forty-eight different parts. When (or if) you had collected all forty-eight cards, these could be sent off to Wills and they would send you a print of the actual picture, such as 'The Laughing Cavalier' or 'The Boyhood of Raleigh' and so forth. Anstie, Ardath and various other manufacturers also issued these sectional series.

Probably the most weird and wonderful sectional series was Wills 'Animalloys'. These made up an animal in three different sections, but by switching the sections around one can create all kinds of mutations besides the conventional sixteen species which the set made up into.

Carreras issued many sets (some of them very appealing) which made up into games such as 'Happy Families', 'The Greyhound Racing Game' and 'Alice in Wonderland'.

Many of these ingenious ideas have not survivied the test of time as being collectable cards, whereas the more attractive ones are much sought after. To sum up, most cards possess sufficient appeal in themselves to collectors, but one cannot deny the seemingly endless range of novelties and novel ideas. The mind boggles at the inventiveness, yes, and even the eccentricity of those remarkable cards. In short you could say, "you name it – they did it."

(VII)

TRADE CARDS

Other industries apart from the tobacco companies saw the lucrative possibilities of picture cards with their products, and trade cards are one of the first mysteries that a new collector is likely to encounter. I have long lost count of the number of times a new customer has asked me the meaning of the term 'trade cards'.

In short, they are cards issued with a wide range of commodities other than cigarettes. But there is, however, in the main a vast difference between them and cigarette cards. Whereas the majority of the latter were produced with painstaking attention to detail and accuracy in both picture and text, these standards are sadly lacking where most trade cards are concerned. They are generally inferior in quality, often poorly printed on thinner card, and in many cases the text on the back is vague or inaccurate. Even the pictures leave much to be desired. For example, collectors often comment that many of the sets bear little if any resemblance to the characters they are supposed to depict. There is a very good reason for this. Cigarette cards were marketed for adults. This was inevitable since they were issued with cigarettes, whereas trade cards are mainly issued with products which are aimed at the juvenile market. This all boils down to the fact that very few collectors bother with trade cards and those who do are very selective, choosing only to pursue the better produced pre-war sets such as Fry's, Typhoo Tea and Leibig. Post 1945 trade sets usually being restricted to the better printed sports sets.

CIGARETTE CARD NOVELTIES

RAMBLER ROSE.
(Pleasure; Pain.)

" The birds are glad ; the brier-
 rose fills
The air with sweetness ; all
 the hills
Stretch green to June's un-
 clouded sky."—*Whittier.*

The Rambler Rose is closely
identified with the Wild Rose which
was known in England in olden times
as the Eglantine.

There is an enormous variety of
delightful Rambler Roses—some
summer flowering, some autumn
flowering—but most of the beautiful
hybrids seen in our gardens to-day
are derived from the Wichuraiana,
introduced to this country from
Japan some 50 years ago.

In ancient Persia, the Wild
Rose was the flower of the nightin-
gale. It was believed that the bird
uttered a plaintive cry whenever a
Rose was plucked.

In astrology a Red Rambler
Rose is under the dominion of
Jupiter.

**WIX WOVEN SILK FLOWERS
SET 1945**

**OGDENS "BIRD'S EGGS"
(CUT OUTS)
SET 1050**

**CARRERAS
SET 2929**

**WILLS "ANIMALLOYS" SET 1210
SECTIONAL SERIES**

Of course, when all is said and done the simple golden rule is to collect what appeals to you personally. But a word of warning. A common fallacy is that the value of poorly produced and badly printed trade cards will appreciate with the passing of time in the same way as cigarette cards. This is very unlikely and we would strongly advise collectors not to pay high prices for them. A simple test is that if you are purchasing trade cards from a dealer, try offering similar surplus trade cards back at, say, fifty percent of the price and see how keen they are to buy them.

(VIII)

CIGARETTE CARD STORING AND CONCLUSION

Now let us consider the best ways of housing your cigarette card collection. By far the most popular way is with the modern loose-leaf type album with transparent leaves, enabling both front and back of the cards to be displayed. These have many advantages over the pre-war albums. Once the cards are placed into the leaves there is little danger of them being damaged. It is far simpler to wipe off a sticky finger mark from a plastic sheet than off the cards as would have been the case with all original albums. Another big advantage is that leaves of varying sizes can be included in the same albums, whereas the old albums were very restrictive. It is generally considered that one of the main reasons for the vast increase in the number of collectors over the past decade is due to the introduction of these albums.

There are a number of different ways in which collectors prefer to arrange their sets in the albums. Some list them in alphabetical order under the makers. Others prefer to display them in chronological order, whereas still others assemble them in groups of the same subject matter, thus virtually converting the collection into a set of encyclopaedias.

But whatever method a collector chooses to adopt it is inevitable that from time to time he will wish to change his cards around, and this is probably the greatest advantage of all with the loose-leaf album, for with the old type album, once the cards had been secured in them there was always the risk of damaging them very badly when removing them. With the modern album one only has to remove the page and replace it where desired.

To further enhance the appearance of the collection the black backing sheets which interleave between the loose leaves do wonders for the presentation of the cards. Further details of albums can be found on page 10 and 11.

Prior to the introduction of this type of album the serious collector normally had two choices. To keep his cards in containers such as cigarette packets or to make his own albums as the three main types of albums issued by the manufacturers were all frowned upon for, in one way or another, damaging the cards. These 'notorious' albums were the 'cross-member' type, the 'slip-in' and the 'stick-in'.

Another method of displaying cards which has become increasingly popular over the last few years is to frame them. These can make very attractive wall displays, setting the cards off admirably as well as preserving their fine condition. To satisfy the needs of the collector who wishes to display his cards in this manner we have devised a frame which in no way damages the cards, yet displays them both front and back. The method is quite simple. We sell cut-out mounting boards that are cut accurately to the size of the cards, both in standard size and the large Player's size. The mounting board is then glued onto a sheet of glass, the cards then positioned in the cut-out mount and a second piece of glass placed on top. The frame is then fixed around this in the normal manner and the cards are displayed back and front without any damage whatsoever. The only thing to bear in mind is that they should not be placed in the sunlight. Details and prices of mounting boards and complete kits can be found on page 12.

CIGARETTE CARD NOVELTIES

ARDATH COUPON

INTERNATIONAL TOBACCO CO.
METAL PLAQUE

CAVANDERS
STEREOSCOPIC CARDS

HILLS SET 713 PRINTED ON CANVAS
(CARTOPHILIC TERM SILK)

CAVANDERS HAND PAINTED
VIEWS

GODFREY PHILLIPS
SILK SET 365

The introduction of this type of framing kit has proved to be very popular, even with the most conventional of collectors. But in the final analysis the only person who can decide how you wish to display your cards is yourself.

But a word of caution. There are, sad to say, unscrupulous dealers around who simply buy up cheap, dirty cards with damaged backs, glue them into frames and sell them for astronomical prices on the pretext of being investments. Needless to say this practice is abhorred by both serious collectors and reputable dealers alike.

Most collectors will agree that there is little point in building up a collection of cards only to entomb them in boxes or a drawer. The serious collector of yesteryear often had little alternative but to resort to this method, and we have experienced many an old-time collector who has gone over to the modern forms of displaying cards, and the joy of seeing his collection presented in an attractive manner has virtually given him a new lease of life.

I vividly remember one old gentleman who told me that he had been collecting cigarette cards for over fifty years and had never done anything else with his sets other than put them into rows in drawers. How, he asked me, could he possibly afford to purchase albums sufficient enough to house his large collection?

During the course of our conversation he revealed to me that he had many duplicate sets and a mutually beneficial arrangement was arrived at. Every Friday he would turn up with a little box of cards and we would negotiate a transaction. Then off he would go with two carrier bags full of albums. He would usually have an interesting little story to tell me about how he had acquired certain sets, and it was sheer joy to see the pleasure he received from seeing those sets displayed in the albums.

Cigarette card collecting has certainly come a long way since its beginnings. Far from fading into obscurity the collecting of cigarette cards has flourished and increased tremendously. After all, they do offer a welcome escape from the rat-race. No 'A' or 'O' levels are necessary either. They are more than just cards with pictures on. They are works of art – and what value they present! A splendid collection of pocket-size reference books – and a conveniently small pocket, too! And fifty percent of these 'reference books' are illustrated, and the text – the other fifty percent – is terse but informative, with all the usual padding and irrelevancies removed.

It would be quite fair to say that cigarette cards are representative of all aspects of the history and growth of our world and human life, and the better aspects of it, too. They present all facets of virtually every subject known to mankind.

Should ever a carefully chosen selection of cigarette cards be placed in a space capsule and launched into space, eventually to be found by alien beings, I feel quite confident that they would have a most constructive and accurate history of the human race.

JOHN ALBERT WOOSTER

INDEX OF TOBACCO BRAND NAMES

BRAND	TOBACCO COMPANY
Admiral Cigarettes	National Cigarette & Tobacco Co.
Airmail Cigarettes	R & J Hill Ltd.
Albert Cigarettes	British American Tobacco Co. Ltd.
All Arms Cigarettes	Ray & Co. Ltd.
S. Anargyros	American Tobacco Company
Bandmaster Cigarettes	Cohen Weenen & Co. and Major Drapkin & Co.
B.D.V. Cigarettes	Godfrey Phillips
Between the Acts	American Tobacco Company
Big Gun Cigarettes	W. Sandorides & Co. Ltd.
Big Run Cigarettes	American Tobacco Company
Black Cat Cigarettes	Carreras Ltd.
Black Spot Cigarettes	Scerri
Blue Bells	J & F Bell Ltd.
Blush of Day Cigarettes	Robinson & Barnsdale Ltd.
Borneo Queen Cigarettes	B. Morris & Sons Ltd.
Borneo Whiffs	Adcock & Son Ltd.
Bound To Win	H. Archer & Co.
British Consuls	W C Macdonald Inc.
Broadleaf Cigarettes	American Tobacco Company
Broadway Novelties	Teofani & Co. Ltd.
The Buffs	Major Drapkin & Co.
Burline Mixture	Felix Berlyn
Cairo Monopol Cigarettes	American Tobacco Company
Cake Walk Cigarettes	M. Pezaro & Son
Caps The Lot	Bewlay & Co. Ltd.
Carabinier	R. Benson Ltd.
Carlton	Wm. Clarke & Son
Carolina Brights	American Tobacco Company
Casket Cigarettes	J A Pattreiouex Ltd.
Chairman Cigarettes	R J Lea Ltd.
The Challenge Flat Brilliantes	R P Gloag & Co.
Citamora Cigarettes	R P Gloag & Co.
Clifton	Bocnal Tobacco Co.
Club Member Cigarettes	J A Pattreiouex Ltd.
Club Mixture Tobacco	The Continental Cigarette Factory
Colin Campbell Cigars	Robinson & Barnsdale Ltd.
Cooltipt	Abdulla
Copain Cigarettes	British American Tobacco Co. Ltd.
Cork Belted	Wm. Clarke & Son

BRAND	TOBACCO COMPANY
Corktip	Bocnal Tobacco Co.
Coronet Cigarettes	Sniders & Abrahams Pty. Ltd.
Critic Cigarettes	J A Pattreiouex Ltd.
Crowfoot Cigarettes	R & J Hill Ltd.
Cycle Cigarettes	American Tobacco Company
Cymax Cigarettes	A & J Coudens Ltd.
Derby Little Cigars	American Tobacco Company
De Reszke Cigarettes	J Millhoff & Co. Ltd. and Godfrey Phillips
Domino Cigarettes	British American Tobacco Company
Double Ace Cigarettes	Ardath Tobacco Co. Ltd.
Egyptienne Luxury	American Tobacco Company
Eldona Cigars & Cigarettes	Major Drapkin & Co. and J. Millhoff & Co. Ltd.
Emblem Cigarettes	American Tobacco Company and Westminster Tobacco Co. Ltd.
Empress Cigarettes	Burstein Isaacs & Co.
Epaulet	Wholesale Tobacco Company
Erinmore Cigarettes	Murray, Sons & Co. Ltd.
Explorer Cigars	Major Drapkin & Co. and J. Millhoff & Co. Ltd.
F. Farrugia Malta	The Omega Cigarette Factory
The Favourite (Magnums) Cigarettes	Teofani & Co. Ltd.
Festival	Adcock & Son Ltd.
Fez Cigarettes	American Tobacco Company
The Flor de Dindigul Cigar	Bewlay & Co. Ltd.
Forecasta	B. Morris & Sons Ltd.
Four Square	George Dobie & Son Ltd.
Fresher Cigarettes	R. S. Challis & Co. Ltd.
Fume Emblem	Westminster Tobacco Co. Ltd.
Gainsborough Cigarettes	Cohen Weenen & Co.
Gibson Girl Virginia	R & J Hill Ltd.
Gold Coin Tobacco	D. Buchner & Co.
Gold Flake	R & J Hill Ltd.
Gold Leaf	Bewlay & Co. Ltd.
Golden Butterfly	Hignett Bros. & Co.
Golden Cloud	Cope Bros. & Co. Ltd.
Golden Grain	Brown & Williamson Tobacco Corp.
G.P.	Godfrey Phillips
The Greys Cigarettes	United Kingdom Tobacco Co. Ltd.
Greys Tobacco	Major Drapkin & Co.
Guards Cigarettes	Carreras Ltd.

INDEX OF TOBACCO BRAND NAMES CONT.

BRAND	TOBACCO COMPANY
Guiding Star	Major Drapkin & Co.
Hassan Cigarettes	American Tobacco Company
Havana Mixture	J.H. Clure & Son
Havelock Cigarettes	W.D. & H.O. Wills
Hawser	Wholesale Tobacco Company
Heart's Delight Cigarettes	Pritchard & Burton
Helmar Cigarettes	American Tobacco Company
Herbert Tareyton Cigarettes	American Tobacco Company
Hindu Cigarettes	American Tobacco Company
Hoffman House Magnums	American Tobacco Company
Honest Long Cut	W. Duke, Sons & Co. and American Tobacco Company
Honeycomb	Adkin & Sons
Honey Flake	Wholesale Tobacco Company
Hustler Little Cigars	American Tobacco Company
Islander, Fags, Specials, Cubs	Bucktrout & Co. Ltd.
Jack Rose Little Cigars	American Tobacco Company
Jersey Lily Cigarettes	Wm. Bradford
Job	Societe Job
Jockey Club	Cope Bros. & Co. Ltd.
Junior Bar	J. A. Pattreiouex
Junior Member Cigarettes	J. A. Pattreiouex
Just Suits Cut Plug	American Tobacco Company
Kenilworth	Cope Bros. & Co. Ltd.
Kensitas Cigarettes	J. Wix & Sons Ltd.
Klondyke	Edwards, Ringer & Bigg
Kopec Cigarettes	American Tobacco Company
Laurel	Major Drapkin & Co.
Lenox Cigarettes	American Tobacco Company
Le Roy Cigars	L. Miller & Sons
Levant Favourites	B. Morris & Sons Ltd.
Lifeboat Cigarettes	The United Tobacco Companies (South) Ltd.
Life Ray Cigarettes	Carreras Ltd.
Little Rhody Cut Plug	Geo. F. Young & Bro.
Lotus Cigarettes	The United Tobacco Companies (South) Ltd.
Lucana Cigarettes	W. Sandorides & Co. Ltd.
Lucky Strike Cigarettes	American Tobacco Company
Luxury Cigarettes	American Tobacco Company
Madcap	Adkin & Sons
M.F.H.	H. Archer & Co.

189

INDEX OF TOBACCO BRAND NAMES CONT.

BRAND	TOBACCO COMPANY
Magpie Cigarettes	J.J. Schuh Tobacco Co. Pty. Ltd.
Manikin Cigars	J.J. Freeman & Co.
Mascot Cigarettes	British American Tobacco Co. Ltd.
Matossian (Tabacs et Cigarettes Matossian)	Henly & Watkins Ltd.
Max Cigarettes	A. & M. Wix
May Blossom Cigarettes	Lambert & Butler
Mecca Cigarettes	American Tobacco Company
Millbank Cigarettes	Imperial Tobacco Company of Canada Ltd.
Mills Cigarettes	Amalgamated Tobacco Corporation Ltd.
Milo Cigarettes	Sniders & Abrahams Pty. Ltd.
Miners Extra Smoking Tobacco	American Tobacco Company
Mogul Cigarettes	American Tobacco Company
Monastery	Adkin & Sons
Murad Cigarettes	American Tobacco Company
Nebo Cigarettes	American Tobacco Company
New Orleans Tobacco	J. & T. Hodge
Obak Cigarettes	American Tobacco Company
Officers Mess Cigarettes	African Tobacco Manufacturers
OK Cigarettes	African Tobacco Manufacturers
Old Gold Cigarettes	American Tobacco Company
Old Judge Cigarettes	Goodwin & Co.
Old Mills Cigarettes	American Tobacco Company
Old Ships	Dominion Tobacco Co. (1929) Ltd.
One of the Finest	D. Buchner & Co.
Oracle Cigarettes	Tetley & Sons
Our Little Beauties	Allen & Ginter
Oxford Cigarettes	American Tobacco Company
Pan Handle Scrap	American Tobacco Company
Perfection Cigarettes	American Tobacco Company
Peter Pan Cigarettes	Sniders & Abrahams Pty. Ltd.
Pibroch Virginia	C. Fryer & Sons Ltd.
Picadilly Little Cigars	American Tobacco Company
Pick-Me-Up Cigarettes	Major Drapkin & Co. and J. Millhoff & Co. Ltd.
Piedmont Cigarettes	American Tobacco Company
Pilot	Hignett Bros. & Co.
Pinhead Cigarettes	British American Tobacco Co. Ltd.
Pinnace	Godfrey Phillips
Pioneer Cigarettes	The Richmond Cavendish Co. Ltd.
Pirate Cigarettes	W.D. & H.O. Wills

INDEX OF TOBACCO BRAND NAMES CONT.

BRAND	TOBACCO COMPANY
Polo Bear Cigarettes	American Tobacco Company
Polo Mild Cigarettes	Murray, Sons & Co. Ltd.
Private Seal Tobacco	Godfrey Phillips
Puritan Little Cigars	American Tobacco Company
Purple Mountain Cigarettes	W.D. & H.O. Wills
Recruit Little Cigars	American Tobacco Company
Red Cross	P. Lorillard Co. and American Tobacco Co.
Reina Regenta Cigars	B. Morris & Sons Ltd.
Richmond Gem Cigarettes	Allen & Ginter
Richmond Straight Cut Cigarettes	American Tobacco Company
Roseland Cigarettes	Glass & Co.
Royal Bengal Little Cigars	American Tobacco Company
R.S.	The Robert Sinclair Tobacco Co. Ltd.
Ru Faza	Major Drapkin & Co.
St. Dunstans Cigarettes	Carreras Ltd.
St. Leger Little Cigars	American Tobacco Company
Scots Cigarettes	African Tobacco Manufacturers
Scrap Iron Scrap	American Tobacco Company
Senator Cigarettes	Scerri
Senior Service Cigarettes	J.A. Pattreiouex Ltd.
Sensation Cut Plug	P. Lorillard Co.
Shantung Cigarettes	British American Tobacco Company
Silko Cigarettes	American Tobacco Company
Silver Cloud	Hignett Bros. & Co.
Smile Away Tobacco	Carreras Ltd.
Solace	Cope Bros. & Co. Ltd.
Sovereign Cigarettes	American Tobacco Company
Spanish Puffs	H. Mandelbaum
Spinet Cigarettes	R. & J. Hill Ltd.
Spotlight Tobaccos	R. & J. Hill Ltd.
Springbok Cigarettes	The United Tobacco Companies (South) Ltd.
Stag Tobacco	American Tobacco Company
Standard Cigarettes	Carreras Ltd. and Sniders & Abrahams Pty. Ltd.
State Express Cigarettes	Ardath Tobacco Co. Ltd.
Sub Rosa Cigarros	American Tobacco Co.
Sultan Cigarettes	American Tobacco Co.
Summit	International Tobacco Co. Ltd.
Sunripe Cigarettes	R. & J. Hill Ltd.
Sunspot Cigarettes	Themans & Co.
Sweet Caporal	Kinney and American Tobacco Co.

BRAND	TOBACCO COMPANY
Sweet Lavender	Wm. S. Kimball & Co.
Tatley Cigarettes	Walkers Tobacco Co. Ltd.
Teal Cigarettes	British American Tobacco Co. Ltd.
Three Bells Cigarettes	J. & F. Bell Ltd.
Three Castles Cigarettes	W.D. & H.O. Wills
Tiger Cigarettes	British American Tobacco Company
Tipsy Loo Cigarettes	H.C. Lloyd & Son Ltd.
Tokio Cigarettes	American Tobacco Company
Tolstoy Cigarettes	American Tobacco Company
Trawler Cigarettes	J.A. Pattreiouex Ltd.
Trumps Long Cut	Moore & Calvi
Turf Cigarettes	Carreras Ltd.
Turkey Red Cigarettes	American Tobacco Company
Turkish Trophy Cigarettes	American Tobacco Company
Twelfth Night Cigarettes	American Tobacco Company
Two Roses	James Rigg & Son
U.S. Marine	American Tobacco Company
Uzit Cigarettes	American Tobacco Company
Vanity Fair Cigarettes	Wm. S. Kimball & Co.
Vice Regal Cigarettes	W.D. & H.O. Wills
Virginia Brights Cigarettes	Allen & Ginter
Wings Cigarettes	Brown & Williamson Tobacco Corp.
Zira Cigarettes	American Tobacco Company

NOTES